Austin Dobson

Hogarth

Austin Dobson

Hogarth

ISBN/EAN: 9783337129637

Printed in Europe, USA, Canada, Australia, Japan

Cover: Foto ©ninafisch / pixelio.de

More available books at **www.hansebooks.com**

ILLUSTRATED BIOGRAPHIES OF

THE GREAT ARTISTS.

WILLIAM HOGARTH.

ILLUSTRATED BIOGRAPHIES OF THE GREAT ARTISTS.

*The following volumes, each illustrated with from 14 to 20 Engravings, are now ready, price 3s. 6d. Those marked with an **asterisk** are 2s. 6d.*

SIR JOSHUA REYNOLDS. By F. S. PULLING, M.A.
WILLIAM HOGARTH. By AUSTIN DOBSON.
GAINSBOROUGH AND CONSTABLE. By G. BROCK-ARNOLD, M.A.
LAWRENCE AND ROMNEY.* By Lord RONALD GOWER, F.S.A.
TURNER. By COSMO MONKHOUSE
SIR DAVID WILKIE. By J. W. MOLLETT, B.A.
SIR EDWIN LANDSEER. By F. G. STEPHENS.

GIOTTO. By HARRY QUILTER, M.A.
FRA ANGELICO AND BOTTICELLI. By C. M. PHILLIMORE.
FRA BARTOLOMMEO AND ANDREA DEL SARTO. By LEADER SCOTT.
MANTEGNA AND FRANCIA. By JULIA CARTWRIGHT.
GHIBERTI AND DONATELLO.* By LEADER SCOTT.
LUCA DELLA ROBBIA AND CELLINI.* By LEADER SCOTT.
LEONARDO DA VINCI. By Dr. J. PAUL RICHTER.
MICHELANGELO BUONARROTI. By CHARLES CLÉMENT.
RAPHAEL. By N. D'ANVERS.
TITIAN. By R. F. HEATH, M.A.
TINTORETTO. By W. R. OSLER.
CORREGGIO.* By M. COMPTON HEATON.

VELAZQUEZ. By E. STOWE, M.A.
MURILLO.* By ELLEN E. MINOR.

ALBRECHT DÜRER. By R. F. HEATH, M.A.
THE LITTLE MASTERS OF GERMANY. By W. B. SCOTT.
HANS HOLBEIN. By JOSEPH CUNDALL.
OVERBECK. By J. BEAVINGTON ATKINSON.

REMBRANDT. By J. W. MOLLETT, B.A.
RUBENS. By C. W. KETT, M.A.
VAN DYCK AND HALS. By P. R. HEAD, B.A.
FIGURE PAINTERS OF HOLLAND. By Lord RONALD GOWER, F.S.A.

CLAUDE LORRAIN. By OWEN J. DULLEA.
WATTEAU. By J. W. MOLLETT, B.A.
VERNET AND DELAROCHE. By J. RUUTZ REES.
MEISSONIER.* By J. W. MOLLETT, B.A.

"*The whole world without Art would be one great wilderness.*"

HOGARTH

BY AUSTIN DOBSON.

LONDON
SAMPSON LOW, MARSTON, SEARLE, & RIVINGTON
(LIMITED)
ST. DUNSTAN'S HOUSE, FETTER LANE, FLEET STREET, E.C.
1890.

PREFACE.

BY way of preface to this brief account of Hogarth's life and works, it is only necessary to say that all the authorities named in the following list—most of them collected during many years' patient admiration of this great artist's genius—have been diligently consulted in preparing it. Those which may be fairly described as "recent" are, it will be seen, but few in number. To the most considerable of these, however, the Author desires to make especial reference. No one who may hereafter work at Hogarth on a large scale will be able to neglect the mass of minute information which has been brought together in Mr. F. G. Stephens' "Catalogue of the Satirical Prints and Drawings in the British Museum;" and when the next portion, carrying the chronicle from 1761 onwards, shall have been issued, it will be practically useless to consult any antecedent work for information respecting the history and production of those of Hogarth's engravings which are covered by the scheme of the series. This being so, the Author has of necessity gratefully availed himself, for purposes of revision and correction, of the volumes already published.

The Author has also to express his thanks to the

Treasurer of the Honourable Society of Lincoln's Inn for his obliging permission to print the hitherto unpublished letter at pp. 72-3 respecting *Paul before Felix;* and to Messrs. Smith and Elder and the proprietors of the "Pictorial World" for allowing him to make use of the woodcuts which appear in the volume. He is moreover indebted to Mr. G. W. Reid, the Keeper of the Prints at the British Museum, and Mr. R. F. Sketchley, the Librarian of the Dyce and Forster Collections at South Kensington, for much kind and courteous assistance.

In conclusion, it is proper to state that some of the descriptions of the prints have been reproduced, with but little variation, from such of the commentaries to Messrs. Bell and Daldy's "Hogarth" of 1872 as were contributed to that work by the Author.

A. D.

13, Grange Park,
Ealing.

CONTENTS.

CHAPTER I.
INTRODUCTORY	Page 1

CHAPTER II.
BIRTH, EDUCATION, AND EARLY YEARS . . . 7

CHAPTER III.
THE TWO PROGRESSES 19

CHAPTER IV.
HISTORY-PICTURES AND MINOR PRINTS 33

CHAPTER V
THE "MARRIAGE-A-LA-MODE". 47

CHAPTER VI.
CONTEMPORARIES, "MARCH TO FINCHLEY," MINOR PRINTS . 61

CHAPTER VII.
"THE ANALYSIS," "ELECTION PRINTS," AND "SIGISMONDA". 75

CHAPTER VIII.
WILKES AND CHURCHILL, DEATH, CONCLUSION . . . 91

CHRONOLOGY OF HOGARTH'S LIFE	111
A LIST OF ENGRAVINGS BY AND AFTER HOGARTH . . .	113
A LIST OF THE PRINCIPAL PAINTINGS BY HOGARTH . .	121
ORIGINAL PRICES OF HOGARTH'S PRINTS	124
INDEX	126

LIST OF ILLUSTRATIONS.

	Page
William Hogarth . . . . . . *To face title*	
Group from " Rake's Progress "	26
,, ,, " Southwark Fair ".	30
,, ,, " Midnight Modern Conversation " . . .	36
The Distrest Poet	44
Group from " The Enraged Musician "	46
,, ,, " Marriage-à-la-Mode " (Pl. i.) . . .	50
,, ,, ,, ,, (Pl. iv.) . . .	56
" Simon Lord Lovat "	64
" Industry and Idleness " (Pl. v.)	68
Group from " Calais Gate "	70
Frontispiece to Kirby's Perspective	80
Group from " Election Prints "	82
" The Bathos "	98
" A Pleased Audience at a Play "	115
Group from " March to Finchley " . .	118

WOODCUTS.

Ellis **Gamble's** Shop-Card	9
Tail-piece **to** Hogarth's " Tour "	18
Hogarth's Tomb at Chiswick	101
Hogarth's Book-Plate	112

[*The photographic reproductions* in *this Volume are taken from carefully-selected impressions of Hogarth's* **original prints** *in the Dyce and Forster Collections at South Kensington.*]

BIBLIOGRAPHY.

A List of the principal works on Hogarth.

[ROUQUET —.] Lettres de Monsieur * * à un de ses Amis à *Paris*, pour lui expliquer les Estampes de Monsieur *Hogarth*. Londres, 1746. (Explains the two *Progresses, Marriage-à-la-Mode,* and the *March to Finchley.*)

TRUSLER, Rev. JOHN. *Hogarth Moralized.* London, 1768. ("With the approbation of *Jane Hogarth*, Widow of the late Mr. Hogarth.")

WALPOLE, HORACE. Anecdotes of Painting in England. **Vol.** iv. London, 1780.

[NICHOLS, JOHN, and STEEVENS, GEORGE.] Biographical Anecdotes of William Hogarth. London, 1781. 2nd Edition, 1782; **3rd** Edition, 1785.

[—FELTON] An Explanation of several of Mr. Hogarth's Prints. London, 1785.

IRELAND, JOHN. Hogarth Illustrated. 2 vols. London, 1791.

IRELAND, SAMUEL. Graphic Illustrations of Hogarth. 2 vols. London, 1794-9.

LICHTENBERG, GEORG CHRISTOPH. Ausführliche Erklärung der Hogarthischen Kupferstiche. Gottingen, 1794-1816.

IRELAND, JOHN. A Supplement to Hogarth Illustrated; compiled from his original Manuscripts. London, 1798. (This is "vol. iii. and last" of Hogarth Illustrated, *v. supra.*)

COOK, THOMAS. **Anecdotes of the celebrated** William Hogarth, **&c.** London, 1803. (Includes the *Analysis of Beauty.*)

NICHOLS, JOHN, **and STEEVENS,** GEORGE. The Genuine Works of William **Hogarth.** 3 vols. London, **1808-17.** (The basis of this book is the "Biographical **Anecdotes.**" The third **volume** includes the so-called "Clavis Hogarthiana," by **the Rev. E.** Ferrers, and the "Five Days' Tour" printed by Rd. Livesay in 1782.)

CUNNINGHAM, ALLAN. Lives of the most eminent British Painters. Vol. i. London, **1829.**

[NICHOLS, J[OHN] B[OWYER].] Anecdotes of William Hogarth, written by himself, &c. London, 1833. (Contains the "Essay" of Charles Lamb, Hazlitt on the *Marriage-à-la-Mode,* &c.)

BROWNLOW, JOHN. Memoranda; or Chronicles of the Foundling Hospital, including Memoirs of Captain Coram, &c., &c. London, 1847.

SALA, GEORGE AUGUSTUS. William Hogarth: Painter, Engraver, and Philosopher. Essays on the Man, the Work, and the Time. London, 1866. (Reprinted from the "Cornhill Magazine.")

STEPHENS, FREDERIC **GEORGE.** Catalogue of the Prints and Drawings in the British Museum. **Division I.** Political and Personal Satires. Vol. **ii.,** 1873. Vol. **iii.** (in two **parts),** 1877. **London.**

WILLIAM HOGARTH.

CHAPTER I.

INTRODUCTORY.

THE greatest of our native pictorial satirists has not wanted for commentators and expositors of all sorts, even of those

"who view
In Homer more than Homer knew."

The two earliest—Rouquet the enameller, who described some of the plates for the use of foreigners, and the Rev. Dr. Trusler, who "moralized" the majority of them—are more noteworthy for their respective relations with the painter and the painter's widow than from any especial merit in their performances. Horace Walpole, who followed these, was, on the contrary, a critic of a far higher order. But he reserved his enthusiasm too exclusively for fashionable amateurs like Mrs. Damer and Lady Di. Beauclerk, to do real justice to the plain-spoken artist of Leicester Fields. Georg Christoph Lichtenberg, a German *litté-*

rateur of considerable sagacity, and John Ireland the Westminster printseller were thoroughly sympathetic, and have written exhaustively on their theme; but both are somewhat too prone to use it as a peg on which to hang fantastic and often irrelevant disquisition. The great body of Hogarth fact is to be found in the successive "Anecdotes" of the antiquary and printer John Nichols, and in the volume issued in 1833 by his son, John Bowyer Nichols. In the case of the former, however, considerable allowance must be made for the malice of his assistant and adviser, George Steevens, who, it has been justly said, "seems to have taken a pleasure in mingling his own gall with the honey of his coadjutor's narrative." As to the rest, Samuel Ireland, the author of the "Graphic Illustrations," is rather to be regarded as "a snapper up of unconsidered trifles" than a contributor of real information; while the commentaries to Cook's and Clerk's editions are of little value. Besides these, there are the lively if somewhat inaccurate life by Allan Cunningham,[1] the technically authoritative sketch in Redgrave's "Century of Painters;" and—not to mention some minor names and anonyms—the well-known essays of Charles Lamb, Hazlitt, Thackeray, and James Hannay.[2]

Upon first inspection then, it would appear that enough has been said respecting a subject which has occupied so

---

[1] Recently edited by Mrs. Charles Heaton.

[2] We purposely refer to deceased authors only. But we do not, for this reason, forget the picturesque pages which Mr. Sala—surely the most enthusiastic of modern Hogarthians—contributed to the "Cornhill" in 1860, or the suggestive paper of Mrs. Oliphant in her "Historical Sketches of the Reign of George II." To the later labours of Mr. F. G. Stephens we have already directed attention.

many pens. And, in truth, were a "Hogarth Society" to be founded, it may be doubted whether any material addition could now be made to the slender stock of existing fact respecting the painter's life. It is not likely, for example, that any new light, if new light be needful, will ever be thrown on that disreputable quarrel with Wilkes and Churchill. Nor can it be supposed, because we are able to regard the much-abused *Sigismonda* without the passion that seems to have animated the partisans of the "Black Masters," that anything important will transpire to clear that clouded reputation. Some day, no doubt, a critic, with (or without) the transfiguring enthusiasm of a Sainte-Beuve, will take up the "Analysis," and demonstrate once more that it contains much common-sense and some unregarded truths; but it will scarcely again enter into circulation, or be commended in pompous commonplace by our Warburtons and Hoadlys. Nevertheless, although the main circumstances of the painter's career must remain unaltered, there will always be a side of his work which will need interpretation. Besides painting the faults and follies of his time, he was pre-eminently the pictorial chronicler of its fashions and its furniture. The follies are enduring; but the fashions pass away. In our day—a day which has witnessed the demolition of Northumberland House, the removal of Temple Bar, and we know not what other time-honoured and venerable landmarks—much in Hogarth's plates must seem as obscure as the cartouches on Cleopatra's Needle. Much more is speedily becoming so; and without a guide the student may scarcely venture into that doubtful rookery of tortuous streets and unnumbered houses—the LONDON of the eighteenth century.

WILLIAM HOGARTH.

Were it not beyond the purpose of this modest biographical sketch, it would be a pleasant task to loiter for a while in that passed-away London of Hogarth, of Fielding, of Garrick;—that London of John Rocque's famous map of 1746, when "cits" had their "country-boxes" and "gazebos" at Islington and Hackney, and fine gentlemen their villas at *Marybone* and *Chelsey*; when duels were fought in the "fields" behind the British Museum, and there was a windmill at the bottom of Rathbone Place. We should find the Thames swarming with noisy watermen, and the streets with trotting Irish chairmen; we should see the old dusky oil-lamps lighted feebly with the oil that dribbled on the "Rake" when he went to Court; and the great creaking signs that obscured the sky, and sometimes toppled on the heads of his Majesty's lieges underneath. We should note the filthy kennels and the ill-paved streets; and rejoice in the additional facilities afforded for foot-passengers at the "new buildings near *Hanover* Square (!)" We might watch his Majesty George II. yawning in his Chapel Royal of St. James's, or follow Queen Caroline of Anspach in her walk on Constitution Hill. Or we might turn into the Mall, which is filled on summer evenings with a "*Beau Monde*" of peach-coloured coats and pink *négligées*. But the tour of Covent Garden (with its column and dial in the centre) would take at least a chapter, and the pilgrimage of Leicester Fields another. We should certainly assist at the Lord Mayor's Show; and we might, like better men before us, be hopelessly engulfed in that great westward-faring crowd, which, after due warning from the belfry of St. Sepulchre's, swept down the old Tyburn Road on "Execution Day" to see the last of Laurence Shirley,

Earl Ferrers, or the highwayman James Maclean. It is well, perhaps, that our limits are exactly defined.

Moreover, much that we could do but imperfectly with the pen Hogarth has done imperishably with the graver. Essentially metropolitan in his tastes, there is little notable in the London of his day of which he has not left us some idea. He has painted the Green Park, the Mall, and Rosamond's Pond. He has shown us Covent Garden and St. James's Street, Cheapside and Charing Cross, Tottenham-Court Road, and Hog Lane. He has shown us Bridewell, Bedlam, and the Fleet Prison. Through a window in one print we see the houses on Old London Bridge; in another Temple Bar, surmounted by the ghastly relics of Jacobite traitors. He takes us to a cock-fight in Birdcage Walk, a dissection in Surgeons' Hall. He gives us reception-rooms in Arlington Street, counting-houses in St. Mary Axe, garrets in "Porridge Island," and cellars in Blood-Bowl Alley. He reproduces the decorations of the Rose Tavern or the Turk's Head Bagnio as scrupulously as the monsters at Dr. Misaubin's in St. Martin's Lane, or the cobweb over the poor-box in Mary-le-bone Old Church. The pictures on the walls, the Chinese nondescripts on the shelves, the tables and chairs, the pipes and punch-bowls, nay, the very tobacco and snuff, have all their distinctive physiognomy and prototypes. He gives us, unromanced and unidealized, "the form and pressure," the absolute details and accessories—the actual *mise-en-scène* of the time he lived in.

But he has done much more than this. He has peopled his canvas with its *dramatis personæ*, with vivid types of the more strongly-marked actors in that cynical and sensual, brave and boastful, corrupt and patriotic age.

Not, be it understood, of its Wolfes and Johnsons,—he was a humorist and a satirist, and goodness was no game for his pencil; rather the Lovats and Charteris, the Sarah Malcolms and the Shebbeares. He was a moralist, after the manner of eighteenth-century morality, not savage like Swift, not ironical like Fielding, not tender at times like Johnson and Goldsmith; but unrelenting, uncompromising, uncompassionate. He drew vice and its consequences in a thoroughly literal and business-like way, neither sparing nor softening its details, incapable of flattering it even for a moment, preoccupied only with seizing its exact contortion of pleasure or of pain. In all his delineations, as in that famous design of Prud'hon's, we see Justice and Vengeance following hard upon the criminal. He knew, no doubt, as well as we, that not seldom (humanly speaking) the innocent are punished and the guilty go at large. What matter? that gospel should not be preached—by him at any rate. So he drew his "Bogey" bigger, if possible, and drove his graver deeper.

What antecedents, what progress of circumstance, what special conditions produced this unique and original artist in an era of mediocrities like Knapton and Shackleton, Highmore and William Kent?—in an age given over to auctioneers and art-charlatans, to adventurers like Heidegger of the "Masquerades," to Italian singers and French ballet-dancers? In the chapter that follows he shall speak for himself as far as possible; but when all is said and done, the reader will probably find no more conclusive reply to the question than this—that he was a great and exceptional genius, not to be quite satisfactorily accounted for by any preconceived theory respecting his race, his epoch, or his surroundings.

CHAPTER II.

BIRTH, EDUCATION, AND EARLY YEARS.

1697 TO 1732.

SOME time before the year 1798 John Ireland received from Mrs. Hogarth's cousin and executrix, Mary Lewis, then resident at Chiswick, a number of documents by the painter which had been religiously preserved by his widow. They included the MS. of the "Analysis of Beauty," corrected by the author, and among the rest a brief sketch of his life. Apart from the story of his prints, it was not a very eventful one; but the account of it which he has left is thoroughly characteristic, and throws much interesting light upon his mode of work, and the singular training for his vocation which he appears to have adopted.[1]

His father was a north-countryman, educated at St. Bees, and sometime kept a school. This being unsuccessful, he came to London; and here William Hogarth was born, on the 10th day of November, 1697, and baptized on the 28th of the same month in the church of St. Bartholomew the Great. "My father's pen," he says [Mr. Hogarth, senior,

---

[1] See note to chap. vi. as to these MSS.

was then earning a precarious subsistence as a literary hack and corrector of the press], "like that of many other authors, did not enable him to do more than put me in the way of shifting for myself. As I had naturally a good eye, and a fondness for drawing, *shows* of all sorts gave me uncommon pleasure when an infant; and mimicry, common to all children, was remarkable in me. An early access to a neighbouring painter drew my attention from play; and I was, at every possible opportunity, employed in making drawings. I picked up an acquaintance of the same turn, and soon learnt to draw the alphabet with great correctness. My exercises when at school were more remarkable for the ornaments which adorned them than for the exercise itself."

These circumstances, coupled with the boy's daily experience of "the precarious situation of men of classical education," as illustrated by his father's career, brought his school-days to a premature conclusion. By his own desire he was apprenticed to a "silver-plate engraver," Mr. Ellis Gamble, at the sign of the "Golden Angel," in Cranbourne Street or Alley, Leicester Fields. There is still extant a shop-card engraved by the young apprentice, in which the angel in question poises a bulky palm-branch in a volatile manner over an announcement of Mr. Gamble's dealings in "Plate, Rings, and Jewells," or as the French version has it, with some neglect of orthography,—"*Argenterie, Bagues & Bijouxs.*"

But long ere the expiration of this apprenticeship, the decorating of salvers and tankards with florid heraldic monsters had been found by young Hogarth to be far too limited for his ambition. He felt the inner consciousness of capacity; and craved for something better. The "something better" at first seemed to be "engraving on copper." "Engraving on copper was, at twenty years of age, my utmost ambition." For this, however, he was not sufficiently skilled as a draughtsman. How to find some royal road to this latter attainment, which should not too much

ELLIS GAMBLE'S SHOP-CARD.

interfere with his pleasure (he frankly confesses to this!), was his first endeavour. Drawing from the life was too mechanical; copying (which he learnt to do with tolerable exactness) "little more than pouring water out of one vessel into another"—in short, he was face to face with the problem how to become an artist without going through the usual course of study; or, as one of his colleagues humorously put it, "how to draw well without drawing at all." Here is his reasoning.

"For this purpose, I considered what various ways, and to what different purposes the memory might be applied; and fell upon one which I found most suitable to my situation and idle disposition—laying it down first as an axiom, that he who could by any means acquire and retain in his memory perfect ideas of the subject he meant to draw, would have as clear a knowledge of the figure, as a man who can write freely hath of the twenty-four letters of the alphabet and their infinite combinations (each of these being composed of lines), and would consequently be an accurate designer." To attain the power of making new designs, as opposed to mere copies, was, he says, his first, and greatest ambition. "I therefore endeavoured to habituate myself to the exercise of a sort of technical memory, and by repeating in my own mind, the parts of which objects were composed, I could by degrees combine and put them down with my pencil. Thus, with all the drawbacks which resulted from the circumstances I have mentioned, I had one material advantage over my competitors, viz. the early habit I thus acquired of retaining in my mind's eye, without coldly copying it on the spot, whatever I intended to imitate. Sometimes, but too seldom, I took the life, for correcting the parts I had not perfectly enough remembered, and then I transferred them to my compositions."

"My pleasures and my studies, thus going hand in hand, the most striking objects that presented themselves, either

comic or tragic, made the strongest impression on my mind;
but had I not sedulously practised what I had thus acquired, I should very soon have lost the power of performing it."

As the old French balladist has it, *Il ne faict pas ce tour qui veult.* That this method of study succeeded with Hogarth should not recommend it as an example; and even in his case its disadvantages were always more or less perceptible. It is quite possible too that, looking backward with the complacency of old age (he must have written the above account in the last years of his life), he depreciated his skill to magnify his theory. At all events, the engraving of the *Kendal Arms,* which Ireland has copied, proves that even during his apprenticeship he was no mean designer; and there is a well-known anecdote of a ludicrous picture made in a public-house, about the same period, which testifies to his power of seizing expression.

To return, however, to the story of his life. The passages above apparently refer to the period when his apprenticeship to Ellis Gamble had terminated, as he says he was twenty. He seems at first to have intended to follow the trade to which he had been brought up, for, if we except a snuff-box lid engraved with the *Rape of the Lock* (1717 ?), his earliest work was his own card, decorated with Cupids and inscribed "W. Hogarth, engraver, Aprill ye 23rd, 1720."[1] "His first employment," says Nichols, "seems to have been the engraving of arms and shopbills." From this he passed to "plates for booksellers." Two of the first of these were *An Emblematic Print on the*

---

[1] The dates differ on these cards; but we follow that in the British Museum.

South Sea, and *The Lottery*, both assigned to the year 1721. In a larger work they might demand notice; here we must pass them by. After these, in 1723, came eighteen illustrations to the travels of Aubrey de la Motraye; seven to Briscoe's "Apuleius," 1724; the plate known as *Masquerades and Operas, Burlington Gate*, 1724, which is notable as being the first he published on his own account; five prints for the translation of "Cassandra," 1725; the *Burlesque on Kent's Altar-piece at St. Clement's*, 1725; a frontispiece to the Oxford squib of "Terræ Filius," 1726, and twelve plates to Butler's "Hudibras." Of these last (we **have** omitted to chronicle some lesser pieces, which will **be** found in our final catalogue), only *Masquerades and Operas*, the *Burlesque on Kent*, and the plates to "Hudibras," need more than a passing comment.

Masquerades and Operas, **which Hogarth in** his biographical **notes calls** *The Taste of the Town*, shows how definitely **he had** chosen **his** side at **the** outset. All through his life we shall find him striking **vigorously** at foreign favourites, at quacks and charlatans **of** all kinds, and in this little plate he touches the key-note, as it were, of his future work. Crowds are seen eagerly flocking to the Italian Opera—that "*Dagon* of the Nobility **and** Gentry which had so long seduced them to Idolatry," to the Lincoln's Inn Fields Pantomime of "Dr. Faustus," to Fawkes the Conjuror's "Dexterity of Hand," and to Swiss Heidegger's impure Masquerades; while the neglected folios of Shakespeare, Ben Jonson, and others, are wheeled to the waste-paper shops. On a show-cloth above, the Earl of Peterborough (Swift's *Mordanto*) is on his knees to Francesca Cuzzoni, the singer, who had come to England in the previous year. At the back is the gate of Burlington

House, labelled "Academy of Arts," and surmounted by the figure of Lord Burlington's favourite, the fashionable "Jack-of-all-Trades" William Kent, who has Michael Angelo and Raphael for supporters. This was a personage whom our sturdy satirist might well be expected to hold in utter detestation, and of whom he would be likely to hear little good at Sir James Thornhill's recently opened Art school in Covent Garden, which he now began to attend, upon those rare occasions when he "took the life" to correct his memories.

But the blow he struck at Kent in this lively satire was feeble compared with that which followed, namely,—the burlesque of the Altar-piece with which Kent's evil genius had prompted him to decorate St. Clement's Danes. Already, upon the criticisms of the parishioners, Bishop Gibson had had it taken down, which was humiliating enough, when Hogarth covered it with further ridicule by a print "exactly engraved" from it. It is a very masterpiece of confusion and bad drawing; but not describable in words.[1]

By the illustrations to "Hudibras," "Hogarth," says Ireland, "first became known in his profession," and they are the most considerable of his efforts in this way. But he was too individual to succeed as an interpreter of other men's thoughts, and it is when he deviates most widely from his author that he is most happy. In this case the concluding plates, representing the *Burning of Rumps at Temple Bar*, and the *Procession of the Skimmington*,—i.e. in honour

---

[1] Allan Cunningham implies that Hogarth's print caused the removal of the altar-piece. But—unless we are to regard it as a humourous anticipation—the very inscription on the print itself contradicts this. It is there called the "Celebrated Altar-Piece in St. Clement's Church *which has been taken down* by Order of ye Lord Bishop of London."

of a man who has been beaten by his wife, are the best of the series.

To the years 1727-8 belongs one of those rare occurrences which have survived as contributions to our artist's biography. Among other commissions he appears to have received one from an upholsterer and tapestry worker named Morris, to execute a design on canvas for the *Element of Earth*, which does not suggest anything particularly definite. The price was to be thirty guineas; but Morris, having been told that the designer was "an engraver and no painter," grew dissatisfied with the work beforehand, and finally refused to pay for it. Hogarth, however, holding that the labourer was worthy of his hire, took the matter into the Westminster Court, where on the 28th of May, 1728, the suit was determined in his favour.[1]

He had already discovered that working for the booksellers was not lucrative, and that publishing upon his own account (as he had done in the case of *Masquerades and Operas*) was simply an incentive to plagiarists and piratical printsellers. Probably it was the aspersion thrown by the above trial upon his skill as a painter that now prompted him to turn his efforts to oil-painting, for about this time, as appears from a memorandum among his papers, he began to paint "small conversation pieces, from twelve to fifteen inches high. This (he says), having novelty, succeeded for a few years." We may here briefly enumerate

---

[1] So says Nichols the elder. Allan Cunningham, it is true, implies the contrary. Probably he had only before him the *second* edition of the "Anecdotes" (1782). In the *third* edition of 1785 the account is corrected in the above sense. The point is important, as it has misled other writers into boldly stating that Hogarth had been declared to be "no painter" in a court of law.

his chief works in oil until the end of the year 1732. They were the *Wanstead Assembly;* the *Committee of the House of Commons examining Bambridge,* an infamous warden of the Fleet prison; a scene from Gay's "Beggar's Opera," notable for its portrait of the beautiful "Polly" (Lavinia Fenton) and her future husband the Duke of Bolton; a little picture of *The Politician,* said to be intended for one Mr. Tibson, a laceman in the Strand; and a scene from Dryden's "Indian Emperor."

During all this time we must assume that he preserved his connection, if not with the school in Covent Garden, at least with Sir James Thornhill, who was one of his witnesses in the Morris suit, and whose suffrages he had no doubt gained by his attacks upon Kent. In fact, his relations with some of the family must have been of the closest, for in 1729 he ran away with Sir James's only daughter Jane, to whom he was married on the 23rd of March at old Paddington Church. The lady was twenty and very handsome. She made an admirable wife, and cherished the memory of her husband, whom she long survived, to the day of her death.

"Soon after his marriage," says Nichols, "*Hogarth* had summer-lodgings at *South* Lambeth." Here he made, or improved, the acquaintance of the enterprising Jonathan Tyers, who was at that time preparing to re-open the New Spring Gardens (as Vauxhall was then called) with an entertainment styled a *Ridotto al fresco.* Hogarth appears to have aided him with suggestions for the decoration of the rooms, for which, among others, he painted a poor picture of *Henry VIII. and Anna Bullen.* His designs for *The Four Times of the Day,* a series of later date, were also copied in oil by Frank Hayman for these gardens, of which by a gold ticket *In perpetuam Beneficii memoriam* the gratified proprietor made Hogarth free.

Although he painted much at this time he does not appear to have relinquished the graver, for between 1726 and 1732 he still wrought frontispieces for the booksellers. In the *Large Masquerade Ticket* (1727 ?) he again satirized Heidegger and fashionable depravity. Another **plate, *Rich's Glory*,** seems to us of doubtful authenticity ; **but it** is interesting from its view of old Covent Garden. **Besides** these should be noted the frontispiece to Fielding's *Tom Thumb*, which, it may be, marks the beginning of his lifelong friendship with the great author of "Joseph Andrews;" and the *Man of Taste*, or *Burlington Gate*, 1731. In this **Kent again** appears, supported as before by reclining statues of Raphael and Michael Angelo. **The** diminutive **figure** of Pope on **a** scaffolding is seen vigorously **whitewashing** the gate, and bespattering **the** passers-by, among others Lord Chandos, while Lord Burlington brings the whitewash. This is in **allusion to** Pope's **epistle** to Lord Burlington, in which under the name of "Timon," Lord Chandos and his seat of Canons near Hampstead were held up to ridicule. The print, it would seem, gave great offence to the persons attacked, for the impression is said to have been recalled and the plate destroyed. But Pope, at least, never attempted any open reprisals. Perhaps he was too wise.

This chapter may be fitly closed with a reference to a pleasant holiday jaunt in which Hogarth took part, and to the perpetuating of which his pencil contributed. On an evening at the close of May, 1732, it occurred to certain boon companions at the Bedford Arms Tavern in Covent Garden to improvise an expedition to be entered on forthwith. The travellers were Hogarth, his brother-in-law John Thornhill, Scott the landscape painter, Tothall, a draper in Tavistock Street, and Forrest, an attorney.[1] They started, "each with a shirt in his pocket," down the river to Gravesend. "At Cuckold's Point we sang *St. John*, at Deptford *Pishoken*; and in Blackwall Reach eat hung beef and biscuit, and drank right Hollands." And so forth. It is a cheery record of songs sung and flip-cans emptied; of the jovial and not over-refined jesting of a party of intimate friends playing truant, and relieving the tedium of sight seeing by bolstering matches, hop-scotch, "fighting perukes," and the like. From Gravesend they go to Rochester,—from Rochester to Chatham, Upnor, Hoo and elsewhere; and their doings find a "faithful chronicler" in Forrest, who sets them down gravely "as a burlesque on historical writers recording a series of insignificant events wholly uninteresting to the reader." When, after five days' wandering, they returned, the journal was promptly bound, gilt, and lettered, and read out at the Bedford Arms Club for the edification of the members then present. It is still preserved in the Print Room of the British Museum, having been purchased by the Trustees in 1847 for about £100. The drawings are by Hogarth and Scott, the map by Thornhill. The title-page runs thus: —"An Account/ of what seem'd most Remarkable in the

---

[1] His signature to the "Tour" is "E. Forrest." He was the father of Theodosius Forrest, of George Street, York Buildings, the solicitor to Covent Garden Theatre and the friend of Colman and Garrick. Theodosius Forrest was a good amateur painter, a song-writer, and a sort of notability in his day. In a mezzotint by Nathaniel Hone, dated 1772, he and Grose, the antiquary, appear as a couple of monks. His death took place in 1784, at the age of fifty-six.

Five Days Peregrination/ of the Five Following Persons Viz*t*. Messieurs/ Tothall. Scott, Hogarth, Thornhill and Forrest./ Begun on Saturday May the 27th 1732/ and Finish'd/ On the 31st of the Same Month/. *Abi tu et fac similiter.*— Inscription on Dulwich Colledge Porch." One of Hogarth's friends, Mr. Gostling, a minor canon of Canterbury Cathedral, made a paraphrase of Forrest's prose in Hudibrastic verse. Of this a few copies were struck off by Nichols in 1781 "as a literary curiosity." It is occasionally confused with the prose journal, which was also published by Richard Livesay the engraver in the following year to accompany *facsimiles* of the original illustrations. In 1871, a reprint of both versions, scarcely so good as it should be, was issued by the late John Camden Hotten. It includes several sketches which do not form part of the original tour.

Besides the above there are other relics of Hogarth in the Museum. In the Department of Manuscripts there is a portion of the "Analysis of Beauty," and also a holograph receipt for engravings sold in 1750 to Earl Ferrers, who was executed at Tyburn for the murder of his steward.

TAIL-PIECE TO HOGARTH'S "TOUR."

CHAPTER III.

THE TWO PROGRESSES.

1733 TO 1735.

SINCE his apprenticeship, when it is to be assumed that he lived with Mr. Gamble in Cranbourne Street, we have no hint of Hogarth's dwelling-place, save that stray reference to "summer-lodgings in *South Lambeth.*" In 1733, however, according to the rate-books, he came to the house in Leicester Fields, as the square was then called, which he occupied, with occasional absences at Chiswick, until his death. The house (the last but two on the east side) was what was formerly the northern half of the Sablonière Hotel, now replaced by Archbishop Tenison's schools; and the painter, in that bust of him by Durham which decorates Mr. Albert Grant's glorified enclosure, must be exactly turning his back upon it. It was conspicuous in Hogarth's day for the sign of the "Golden Head," which he had carved from pieces of cork glued together into a similitude of Van Dyck.[1] Here he would be

---

[1] It may still be detected in contemporary views of the square, *e. g.* those of Maurer and Bowles (1753), now exhibited in the Crace Collection at South Kensington. The house must have been a fair one for those days, as it was rated to the poor in 1756 at £60.

conveniently near those genial friends of the "Bedford Arms" when he was minded for a cheerful cup, and "Why should we quarrel for riches," or any of the chirruping ditties contained in that collection by Leveridge of Tavistock Street, for which, in 1727, he had engraved a frontispiece. Not far off, in all probability, was his friend George Lambert, the scene-painter of Covent Garden; while Pine, the engraver, whose "Horace" is still a delight of collectors, had a shop hard by in St. Martin's Lane. Captain Coram, too, the benevolent originator of the Foundling Hospital, would doubtless be his neighbour, as that good man died "at his lodgings near Leicester Square." But Hogarth had not yet, as may be gathered, attained to any great repute with the general public. Mitchell—Sir Robert Walpole's poet—for whom he had designed a plate, had, indeed, addressed him in 1731 as an "eminent History and Conversation Painter."

> "Large families obey your hand;
> *Assemblies* rise at your command;"

says this grateful panegyrist. Yet even in the obituary notice of Sir James Thornhill in the "Gentleman's Magazine" for May, 1734, he is simply referred to as "Mr. *Wm. Hogarth*, admired for his curious Miniature Conversation Paintings," although he had at this date engraved, if not actually published the first of that wonderful gallery of "pictured morals," which (it might be imagined) should have stamped him, once and for all, as an artist distinct and separate from his predecessors and contemporaries. In 1733, however, according to Rouquet, there were only two printshops (!) in London; and the circulation of engravings must have been of the most languid kind.

The series in question, *A Harlot's Progress*, is dated by Nichols 1733-4. The pictures must have been begun soon after the artist's marriage, as the date upon the coffin in the last plate, which is supposed to denote the conclusion of the painting, is Sept. 2nd, 1731. It would have been of considerable interest if we could have learnt what accident of inspiration suggested this particular style to Hogarth. His own account of the matter is too general to be explicit. Portrait-painting, he gives us to understand, was laborious; and to a conscientious man who could not consent (after the manner of your Hudsons and Knaptons, be it understood!) to degrade it into a mere manufacture—"not sufficiently profitable to pay the expenses my family required. I, therefore, turned my thoughts to a still more novel mode, *viz.*, painting and engraving modern moral subjects, a field not broken up in any country or any age." . . . "I wished to compose pictures on canvas, similar to representations on the stage; and farther hope, that they will be tried by the same test, and criticized by the same criterion. Let it be observed that I mean to speak only of those scenes where the human species are actors, and those I think have not often been delineated in a way of which they are worthy and capable. In these compositions, those subjects that will both entertain and improve the mind bid fair to be of the greatest public utility, and must therefore be entitled to rank in the highest class." . . . "I have endeavoured to treat my subject as a dramatic writer;[1] my picture is my stage, and men and women my players, who by means of certain actions and gestures are to exhibit a

---

[1] It is noticeable that in more than one of his prints he speaks of himself as the "author," not the "artist."

dumb show." . . . "This I found was most likely to answer my purpose, provided I could strike the passions, and by small sums from many, by the sale of prints, which I could engrave from my own pictures, thus secure my property to myself."

Here, of course, is his theory; but it leaves us in the dark as to the particular train of suggestion. To a mind so alert, so quick to employ surrounding material, to seize the humorous or satiric physiognomy of the moment, there must have surely been something special that suggested this picture-chronicle of poor Mary Hackabout. Major thinks, indeed, that a paper by Steele in the "Spectator" (No. 266), in which a procuress is shown catechizing a raw country girl, who has come to town in a waggon, may have supplied the initial hint. But this, if it suggested the first plate, need not (although it may) have suggested the entire set. The artist, in any case, takes us farther. From that first enticement into evil paths his heroine passes, through a "Martin's summer" as the mistress of a rich Jew, to "Captain Macheath" and Drury Lane,—to Bridewell and beating hemp,—to Disease and Death,—to a shameful funeral and a forgotten grave. It is all acted out "*coram populo.*" There is no decorous veiling of the catastrophe, no abatement of the miserable detail, no

> "Passing thought
> Of the old days which seem to be
> Much older than any history
> That is written in any book;
> When she would lie in fields and look
> Along the ground through the blown grass
> And wonder where the city was,
> Far out of sight, whose broil and bale
> They told her for a child's tale."

Hogarth had no space for such regretful sentiment. He had a plain and straightforward message to deliver. If you do that, this will follow,—and this,—and this. With such accessories, grotesque or horrible, as may be.

Where the narrator is so direct and matter-of-fact, it is obvious that in this century, at least, his **work** is not quite easy to write about; and there are, it must be frankly confessed, details here over which, as the prints can be consulted, we shall pass without regret. **But some of** the characters—for some of the characters were real persons— require **to be** named. The man at the door and the elderly woman, **in Pl. i.,** undoubtedly represented the infamous Colonel Francis Charteris and the equally infamous Mother Needham, the latter of whom died in 1731, after exposure in the pillory. The magistrate in Pl. iii. is Sir John Gonson, a well-known "harlot-hunting justice;" the wig-box in the same plate is that of James Dalton, a highwayman, who was hanged at Tyburn in 1730. The doctors in Pl. v. are said to be Drs. Misaubin and Ward, two quacks of the period; while the clergyman (!) in Pl. vi. is identified **with a certain dissolute** " chaplain of the Fleet," and the **shrieking woman with** a procuress named Bentley. Of **the numberless minor** details it is here impossible to speak. **But the** attention of the reader may be briefly directed to the destruction caused by the famished horse in Pl. i., the pictures on the walls in Pl. ii., the degradation of Bishop Gibson's " Pastoral letter " in Pl. iii., the Jews-bread used as a fly-trap and the "Anodyne necklace" advertisement in **Pl. v.,** and finally the sprigs of yew for the prevention of infection in the concluding plate.

By some of the commentators this concluding plate (*The Funeral*) has **been** regarded as an anachronism, and even a superfluity. The artist was wiser than his critics. What other epilogue, indeed, to such a life! Conventionalism, no doubt, would have stepped in with its ready tear and faded "Requiescat." But Hogarth scorned Conventionalism, and copied human nature—hard, frivolous, incorrigible. In his experience **harlots were** harlots to the end of **the** chapter—and after. There were no Magdalens among them. **Their** mourning was a mockery; their priest a profligate. He will not even have the child impressed;—how should he be with such a mother? No; **let** him wind up his new top in the foreground. This painter painted life as he saw it; he could and would do no more.

But whether it was from the austerity of the moral, or the **novelty** of the work, *A Harlot's Progress* gave Hogarth **at once** a position as a genius. Even before they were engraved, **the** paintings **reinstated him** in the good graces of his father-in-law, **Sir** James Thornhill, **who** had never forgiven him for running away **with his** daughter. By the contrivance of Lady Thornhill **and Mrs.** Hogarth they were placed **in** the old man's dining-room. He eagerly asked the artist's name, and, on learning it, said, "Very well; the man who can furnish representations like these, can also maintain a wife without a portion"—a speech which was the precursor of reconciliation. This must have taken place before March, 1733, for he appears to have been present when, early in that month, Hogarth painted the portrait of Sarah Malcolm the murderess, afterwards executed in Fleet Street. When, in the same year, the prints were subscribed for (the subscription ticket being **the** clever little plate of *Boys Peeping at Nature*), more than twelve hundred names were inscribed on the artist's book. On the appearance of Pl. iii. the Lords **of** the Treasury trooped to Leicester Fields[1] for Sir John Gonson's portrait. Theophilus Cibber made the story into a pantomime, and some one else into a ballad-opera, called "The Jew Decoy'd;" and it gave rise to numerous pamphlets and poems. It was painted on fan-mounts and transferred to cups and saucers. Lastly, it was freely pirated. There could be no surer sign of its success.

Hogarth had already suffered from depredations of this kind. Copies of his first published plate, *Masquerades and Operas*, had been sold in shops at half price, while the originals were returned upon his hands. His *Harlot's Progress* had been issued by one Kirkall, even before he could get out his own engravings; and Nichols saw no less than eight piratical imitations of it. In 1735, to use his own words, he "applied to Parliament for redress," and obtained an Act (8 Geo. II. *cap.* 13), vesting an exclusive right in designers, and restraining the multiplying of their works without the consent of the artist. It was ill-drawn, but served in a measure to remedy the evil; and Hogarth commemorated his success in a long inscription on the plate entitled *Crowns, Mitres, etc.*, afterwards used as a subscription ticket to the Election series.

The success of *A Harlot's Progress* prompted *A Rake's Progress*, which followed speedily. It must, in fact, have been begun immediately after the earlier paintings were completed, as from an advertisement in "The Country Journal; or, The Craftsman," of December the 29th, 1733, we learn that the artist was then occupied upon the engravings. They were subscribed for in the same year, the

---

[1] Or perhaps to "*Mr. Bakewell's, printseller*, next the *Horn Tavern* in *Fleet St.*"

ticket being the capital little etching, *A Pleased Audience at a Play*, afterwards styled *The Laughing Audience*. As in the other Progress, Hogarth himself christened his chief character. In the first plate, "Tom Rakewell" (the name, Mr. Stephens points out, is as appropriate to the miser-father as the prodigal son) has entered suddenly upon his inheritance. In a jumble of leases, bonds, and the miscellaneous hoardings of avarice, he is being measured for his mourning. Already his attorney plunders him; and he himself begins badly by casting off the poor girl he has ruined while at Oxford.

"*Prodigus aeris,
Sublimis, cupidusque, et amata relinquere pernix,*"

his fortune is written in his face.

The next plate (*The Levée*) transforms the clumsy lad to an awkward man of fashion. His antechamber is thronged with milliners, wig-makers, tailors, and hatters. The "dealers in dark pictures" have equipped him as a connoisseur,—witness the *Judgment of Paris* on the wall. A much bewigged musician is trying over "The Rape of the Sabines" at a harpsichord; a French horn player preludes noisily upon his instrument. He dabbles in Bridgeman's landscape gardening; and maintains one poet, if not two. But the majority of the visitors at his reception are professors of those sterner arts which no gentleman (in 1735) could be without. He must have his cocks at Newmarket, and his racers at Epsom, where "Silly Tom" has won a cup. Essex must instruct him in dancing; Dubois in fencing; and the great Figg himself in quarter-staff.[1]

---

[1] The figures in the plate are said to be portraits of these professors.

Page 26.

THE TWO PROGRESSES.

And lest his proficiency in the two latter sciences should fail to save his skin, he must employ the cut-throat "man-of-honour," who comes recommended by "Wm. Stab." Roistering "bloods," who finish their revels at the "Shakespeare's Head" or the "Rose" by broiling a waiter, or "pinking" a chairman, sometimes require the aid of henchmen like the Captain, when their humorous exploits fall flat on the spectators.

One of these humorous exploits is depicted in Pl. iii. He is there seen drunk at a tavern in Drury Lane, at three in the morning, surrounded by the trophies of a street row, largely supplemented by further devastations of the apartment itself. His companions, mostly recruited from the *simplices nymphæ* of the neighbouring Piazza, are in scarcely better case. One (like Prior's "Kitty") sets the world on fire (in a map). Another spirts brandy in the face of her furious *vis-à-vis*, who threatens her with a knife. A harper is twanging at the door, a beggar-girl sings the "Black Joke." We omit the remaining details of the plate, which are better studied in the commentators.

This is his zenith: in the next scene he enters upon his decline. He is ignominiously arrested for debt in St. James's Street as he is going to Court in a hired chair on Queen Caroline's birthday, also St. David's day, as is indicated by a Welshman with an enormous leek in his hat. Some temporary assistance is rendered to him by the unfortunate girl of Pl. i.; but it is only temporary, for in the plate that follows he is repairing his fortunes by an alliance in old Mary-le-bone Church, then much used for private marriages, with an elderly heiress. The bride is one-eyed, and tremulously exultant; the bridegroom nonchalant and absorbed in the good-looking lady's-maid. The church, which had been recently repaired, and was taken down in 1741, is depicted, no doubt as a fitting frame to the bride, as extremely dilapidated. The Creed has been destroyed by damp; a crack runs through the Ninth Commandment and the poor-box is covered by a cobweb.

Henceforth Tom Rakewell "progresses" at a headlong rate. Pl. vi. shows him in a Covent Garden gaming-house. He has lost all his recently acquired wealth; and flings himself upon the ground in a paroxysm of fury and execration. In allusion to the burning of White's in April, 1733, flames are seen bursting from the wainscot, but the absorbed gamblers take no heed. The next scene is in "The Fleet;" the last in Bedlam. In the one he is a poor distracted wretch, dunned by the gaoler, pestered by the pot-boy, deafened by the rancorous virago, his wife, and crushed by Mr. Manager Rich's letter.—"S^r. I have read y^r Play & find it will not doe." In the other he is an incurable maniac, fettered and dangerous, who tears himself with the heart-rending laugh of the insane.

Our bare outline does but scant justice to this tragical story: and scarcely touches at all upon its affluence of detail. We are told that it did not meet with the success of the *Harlot's Progress*. The causes are not far to seek. It flew at higher social game. It attacked the vices of the man instead of the vices of the woman; and to the vices of the man society is proverbially tender. Then it was longer, and more unequal than its predecessor. Although it rose to a higher level in the later scenes, in the fourth plate it was (for Hogarth) weak and faltering. Indeed, it is —to say the least—unlikely that a poor milliner would carry about sufficient money to relieve a fine gentleman in peril of the tipstaves. Her presence after Pl. i. is an example of that "pathetic fallacy" we hear so much of. Some one, it must be imagined, had remarked upon the want of tenderness in the *Harlot's Progress*, and Hogarth met the objection in the *Rake's Progress* by the introduction of his ruined sweetheart. But her re-appearances are ill-managed, almost *de trop*. She adds little to the effect of the scenes in the prison or the madhouse, and they would suffer nothing by her absence. If the above conjecture be a correct one, this is another of the many instances in which Hogarth was apparently led astray by his importunate advisers.

The plates of the *Rake's Progress* are all dated June 25th, 1735, and bear the words, "According to Act of Parliament," that is, according to Hogarth's Act mentioned above, which came into operation on the 24th. It is probably, as Mr. Stephens points out, the earliest instance of this form of publication, afterwards so common. With the *Rake's Progress* was issued a print of earlier date, which had been kept back to give it the advantages of protection, *i.e.* that known as *The Fair*, or *Southwark Fair*, one of the liveliest of the separate plates, albeit somewhat coarse in execution. This entertainment (or carnival) was suppressed in 1762; but in 1733, when Hogarth drew it, it was diligently frequented, during the fortnight for which it was held, by "persons of all distinctions of both sexes." Its notabilities are faithfully depicted. Elkanah Settle's droll of the "Siege of Troy," as presented at Lee and Harper's booth; the "posture-master" and "curious Indian birds" of Mr. Fawkes the conjuror; the waxwork exhibiting "the whole Court of France;" Müller, or Miller, the Leipzic giant; Violante the tumbler;

Cadman the steeple-flyer;—all these have been carefully set down. The "Fall of Bajazet" at Cibber and Bullock's is humorously illustrated by the collapse of the "parade" in front of the booth; whilst in the crowd a couple of bailiffs arrest a buskined hero from the same company, who, with a beautiful drummeress, is beating up for an audience. But the incident of the plate is inexhaustible, and would take many pages to describe.

Among the other works which belong to this chapter, and have not been hitherto mentioned, is the capital drinking scene, called *A Midnight Modern Conversation*, 1734. Its proper place lies between the two *Progresses*. In this a party of eleven, whose degrees of intoxication are admirably characterized, have finished some two dozen bottles, and, at four in the morning, are commencing a capacious bowl of punch, presided over by a rosy-gilled parson,—the

*"fortem validumque combibonem
Laetantem super amphorâ repletâ"—*

of Vincent Bourne; but who, in real life, has been identified both with the Rev. Cornelius Ford, a dissolute cousin of Dr. Johnson, and the famous Orator Henley.[1] The frontispiece to Carey's "Chrononhotontologos," 1734; the *Cuzzoni, Farinelli, and Heidegger*, 1734; and the *Opera House*, 1735, like the list of presents to Farinelli in Pl. ii.

---

[1] In Bickham's "Musical Entertainer," 2 vols. 1737 ?—a fine old collection of eighteenth-century songs set by "Mr. Handel," "Mr. Carey," "Mr. Festing," "Mr. Leveridge," and others—this plate is used as a heading to a lyric quite in its own spirit, entitled "The Relief; or Pow'r of Drinking." "The Oratorio" appears above another; and the "Rake's Progress" has been freely plagiarized elsewhere. Over two of the songs are good representations of Spring Garden (Vauxhall), and the "New Tunbridge Wells at Islington."

Page 30

of the *Rake's Progress*, show the artist's unconquered antipathy to the foreign favourites, upon whom the British public squandered fortunes "for a shrug or a song." Perhaps it was not natural under the circumstances that he should do justice to Farinelli; but the British public of the day were not so far wrong in their admiration of that most wonderful of sopranos.

Beside the Act against piratical printsellers, no facts of importance in Hogarth's life during this period have been recorded, except the death of his mother in June, 1735, and that of his father-in-law, Sir James Thornhill, in May, 1734. But, if we may judge by the references to him in contemporary writers, his reputation was steadily increasing. From the hendecasyllabics of Vincent Bourne we have already made a quotation. Somervile, the poet, dedicated his "Hobbinol" to him as "the greatest master in the burlesque way ;" and, in 1736, Swift refers to him in the satire of the "Legion Club." But the most genial tribute came to him somewhat later from the pen of Henry Fielding. As it refers solely to the *Progresses*, we may place it here. "I esteem,"—says he in the "Champion"—"the ingenious Mr. *Hogarth* as one of the most useful Satyrists any Age hath produced. In his excellent Works you see the delusive Scene exposed with all the Force of Humour, and, on casting your Eyes on another Picture, you behold the dreadful and fatal Consequence. I almost dare affirm that those two Works of his, which he calls the *Rake's* and *Harlot's Progress*, are calculated more to serve the Cause of Virtue, and for the Preservation of Mankind, than all the *Folio's* of Morality which have been ever written, and a sober Family should no more be without them, than without the *Whole Duty of Man* in their House." Later still he writes on the same theme, in the preface to "Joseph Andrews," "It hath been thought a vast Commendation of a Painter, to say his Figures *seem to breathe;* but surely, it is a much greater and nobler Applause, *that they appear to think.*"

CHAPTER IV.

HISTORY PICTURES AND MINOR PRINTS.

1736 TO 1744.

THE welcome which Hogarth's picture-comedies had received should (it may be supposed) have convinced him that his best means of permanent success lay in this direction. Yet, according to his own account, which, unhappily, it is somewhat difficult to date, it would appear that he had other and different ambitions. His desire was to take rank with the Haymans and Thornhills—to say nothing of artists more ancient and illustrious. "Before I had done anything of much consequence in this walk (*i.e.*, 'painting and engraving modern moral subjects'), I entertained some hopes of succeeding in what the puffers in books call *the great style of history-painting;* so that, without having had a stroke of this *grand* business before, I quitted small portraits and familiar conversations, and, with a smile at my own temerity, commenced history painter, and, on a great staircase at St. Bartholomew's Hospital, painted two Scripture stories, *the Pool of Bethesda* and *the Good Samaritan*, with figures seven feet high. These I presented to the charity, and thought they might serve as a specimen, to show that were there an inclination in England for encouraging historical pictures, such a first essay might prove the painting them more easily attainable than is generally imagined. But as religion, the great promoter of this style in other countries, rejected it in England, I was unwilling to sink into *a portrait manufacturer;* and still ambitious of being singular, dropped all expectations of advantage from that source, and returned to the pursuit of my former dealings with the public at large."

This is, in some respects, a singular utterance. If we accept 1736, which is the date painted upon the staircase of the Hospital, as the date of the *Good Samaritan* and *Pool of Bethesda,* then the "anything of much consequence" seems an odd under-valuation of the two *Progresses* which had made him a name. Seeing, however, that the sentence, " I quitted small portraits and familiar conversations " does not cover these series, it may be that the Bartholomew's Hospital pictures were painted before 1736. But even if we put them back five years, Hogarth would still have painted the *Harlot's Progress,* and the sentence would remain inexplicable, except by attributing to the artist a perverse blindness as to his abilities. Moreover, his " Scripture stories " were a mistake ; and if they were not good in his own day, they are homelier than ever in ours, when the realism of artists like Holman Hunt and Gérôme have imported into our galleries the very atmosphere and types of the East. With the record that they made the painter a governor of the hospital, we may pass over the *Pool of Bethesda* and the *Good Samaritan.*

During the period covered by the present chapter—*i.e.* from 1735 to 1744—Hogarth did not put forth any important series of plates corresponding to the *Rake's* and *Harlot's Progresses.* Indeed, the *Four Times of the Day*

excepted, he did not publish any "series" at all. He was
doubtless maturing and elaborating his masterpiece, the
Marriage-à-la-Mode, which was advertised in April, 1743,
and to which we shall devote the ensuing chapter. But
during this time several separate prints appeared, which
are among the most popular of his works—*e.g.* the *Strolling Actresses dressing in a Barn*, the *Enraged Musician*, the
Distrest Poet. And here we may observe that it is the defect of his biography that it lies almost wholly in the description of his works. To the facts of his life they must
always bear much the same relation in bulk as the commentary of Warton to the "Minor Poems" of Milton, or the
"notes" to the text in an article by Bayle. Lamb said
justly that we "read" his prints, and look at other pictures. He might have added that the type is minute, and
the page is crammed.

The earliest plates belonging to the year 1736 are the
Company of Undertakers or *Consultation of Physicians*, and
the *Scholars at a Lecture*. The first is a whimsical coat-of-arms, composed of doctors "poising their gilt-head canes"
(as in Tennyson's "Princess"), with the motto, "*Et
Plurima Mortis Imago.*" Conspicuous among them in a
harlequin suit ("issuant checkie") is Mrs. Sarah Mapp, a
famous bone-setter or "shape-mistress," who enjoyed a
brief popularity circa 1736-7. The second, a number of
(for the most part) vulgar academical heads, requires no
special notice. *The Company of Undertakers* is dated March.
To the month of April belongs a ticket for Fielding's
benefit in "Pasquin." There is a doubt whether this
be really Hogarth's; but the strokes at political morality
in that "dramatic satire on the times" would have been
so much to the taste of the artist who later designed the

inimitable *Election Prints*, that one is inclined to give him the benefit of any uncertainty. Concerning the *Sleeping Congregation*, which came out in October of the same year, there is no doubt at all. The drowsy auditory are poorly treated; but the Rev. Dr. Desaguiliers, who

"In one lazy tone
Through the long, heavy, painful page drawls on,"

and his pompous clerk, struggling between Morpheus and the ill-guarded attractions of the pretty girl who has fallen asleep with her prayer-book open at "Matrimony," are not to be improved. Whether the divine, once famous for his lectures on Experimental Philosophy in what is now Cannon Row, Westminster, deserved the satire, we do not know. But here, at least, he will certainly soon be able to say in the words of Horace, which have been suggested as a motto for the plate,—" OMNES *composui*."

In 1737 Hogarth was probably at work on the *Four Times of the Day*, the engravings of which were advertised as finished in April, 1738. Nothing of any importance is recorded for the previous year save a very characteristic letter which he addressed, over the signature of "Britophil," to the "St. James's Evening Post," of June 7th, 1737, in defence of Sir James Thornhill, upon whose paintings at Greenwich certain aspersions had been cast by another journal. We quote it from Nichols, who professes to have "correctly transcribed" it. After commenting upon the criticism which condemns an entire work because of some minor and quite immaterial defect (a kind of criticism, by the way, not wholly extinct even in these days), the writer proceeds to a vigorous attack upon his favourite enemies, the "picture-dealers":—

Page 56.

"There is another set of gentry more noxious to the Art than these, and those are your picture-jobbers from abroad,[1] who are always **ready to raise a great** cry in the prints whenever they **think their craft is in** danger; and indeed it is their interest to depreciate every English work, as hurtful to their trade, of continually importing ship-loads of dead Christs, Holy Families, Madona's, and other dismal dark subjects, neither entertaining **nor ornamental;** on which **they scrawl** the terrible cramp **names of some** Italian mastors, and **fix on us** poor Englishmen the character of *universal dupes.* If **a man,** naturally a judge of Painting, **not bigoted** to those **empirics,** should cast his **eye on one of their** sham virtuoso-pieces, he would be very apt to say, 'Mr. Bubbleman, that grand Venus (as you are pleased to call it) has not beauty enough for the character of an English cook-maid.'—Upon which the quack answers, with a confident air, 'O Lord, sir, I find that you are no connoisseur—that picture, I assure you, is in Alesso Baldovinetto's second and best **manner,** boldly painted, and truely sublime; the contour **gracious; the** air **of the head** in **the high** Greek **taste; and a most** divine idea it is.'—Then spitting on an obscure place, and rubbing it **with a dirty handkerchief, takes a** skip to the other end **of the room, and** screams out **in** raptures, ' There is an amazing **touch!** a man should have this picture a twelve-month in his collection before he can discover half its beauties.' The gentleman (though naturally a judge of what is beautiful, yet ashamed to be out of the fashion

---

[1] "An abuse grown to such a height, that the Legislature has endeavoured to put a stop to it, by laying a duty on the importation of foreign pictures."

in judging for himself) with this cant is struck dumb; gives a vast sum for the picture, very modestly confesses that he is indeed quite ignorant of Painting, and bestows a frame worth fifty pounds on a frightful thing, without the hard name on it not worth as many farthings."[1]

We have quoted this passage because it shows that, notwithstanding the sneers cast at the painter's education, he could write forcibly and graphically when his feelings were aroused. If his sketch be not worthy of that immortal genius who defined connoisseurship as consisting in the assertion that the picture might have been better if the painter had taken more pains, and in praising the works of Pietro Perugino—if it be not worthy of Goldsmith, it might well have come from the pen of him who drew that painter Pallet whom Peregrine Pickle met at Paris. It would do no dishonour to the pen of Smollett. No doubt Hogarth's inimical critic, George Steevens, would hint that the letter was probably "corrected" by Hoadly or Ralph, but, in the absence of any such suggestion, we may concede (with Ireland) that it "carries internal evidence of his mind." It will help us to understand the pictures on the walls in Pl. i. of *Marriage-à-la-Mode*, and the future story of *Sigismonda*.

The engravings of the *Four Times of the Day* are dated March 25th, 1738. They represent three scenes in London and one at Islington; and the pictures were, as already stated in chap. ii., originally designed for Mr. Jonathan Tyers of Vauxhall. They are highly interesting, if only as

---

[1] "*e.g.* A monstrous Venus at Kensington, valued at a thousand pounds, said to be painted by Michael Angelo de Buonarotti or Jacomo di Pontermo or Sebastiano del Piambo" (*sic*).

illustrations of the time. The first plate shows us Covent Garden at early morning on a winter's day, with a disorderly company coming out of "Tom King's Coffee House;"[1] the second, a congregation issuing at noon, on Sunday, from the French chapel in Hog Lane, St. Giles's (now Crown Street); the third, a citizen and his wife returning from Sadler's Wells on a sultry summer's evening, and the fourth, the neighbourhood of Charing Cross at night, on "Restoration Day," with the "Salisbury Flying Coach" upset in the middle of a bonfire. The last is the worst of the series, the second is the best; but all are filled with a multiplicity of detail that deserves careful study. The uproarious misery of the lad in *Noon*, who has broken his pie-dish by resting it upon a post, and the delightful coxcombry of the Frenchman in his *ailes-de-pigeon* and *solitaire*, the much-enduring dyer and his melting wife in *Evening*, and the drunken freemason in *Night*, are excellent. But the cream of the characters represented is certainly the censorious old prude in the first scene with her lank-haired and shivering footboy. She is said to have been an aunt of the painter, who, like Churchill, lost a legacy by too crude a frankness. Fielding borrowed her lineaments for the portrait of Miss Bridget Allworthy, and Thackeray has copied her wintry figure for one of the initials to the "Roundabout Papers." To her, too, Cowper has consecrated an entire passage of "Truth."

---

[1] Of Moll King, the then proprietor of this resort and a successful rival of the Needhams and Bentleys of her epoch, Mr. Edward Draper of Vincent Square, Westminster, has a remarkable portrait, ascribed on good authority to Hogarth. In this she appears as a bold, handsome, gipsy-looking woman, holding a cat in her lap. She died in retirement at Hampstead, Sept. 17, 1747.

"Yon ancient prude, whose wither'd features show
She might be young some forty years ago,
Her elbows pinioned close upon her hips,
Her head erect, her fan upon her lips,
Her eyebrows arched, her eyes both gone astray
To watch yon amorous couple in their play,
With bony and unkerchief'd neck defies
The rude inclemency of wintry skies,
And sails with lappet head and mincing airs
Duly at clink of bell to morning prayers.
To thrift and parsimony much inclined,
She yet allows herself that boy behind;
The shivering urchin, bending as he goes,
With slipshod heels and dewdrop at his nose,
His predecessor's coat advanced to wear,
Which future pages yet are doomed to share,
Carries her Bible tuck'd beneath his arm,
And hides his hands to keep his fingers warm."

One of the results brought about by the bitter personalities of Fielding's "Pasquin," **and** its successor the **"Historical Register," was the** passing of that "Act against Strolling Players," which, among **other** things, made it penal to represent plays out of the city and liberties of Westminster for **hire,** gain, or reward. This gave rise to the excellent print which Hogarth issued with the *Four Times of the Day,* viz., *Strolling Actresses dressing in a Barn.* The play **to be** presented is "The Devil to pay in Heaven," a piece which will be vainly sought for in the "Play-House Companions" of the period. It is, however, aptly enough symbolized **by** the plate itself—surely the most humorous assemblage of vaulting pretensions and creeping commonplaces that were ever combined together. In the centre Diana, not much more closely clad than Shakespeare's "chariest maid,"

"If she unmask her beauty to the moon,"

recites (and probably rants) her part. Near to her Flora is tallowing her hair, while Night (a negress) darns a hole in Juno's stocking. Jupiter, "with his red right hand," is peaceably superintending the removal by Cupid of some stockings from the cloud (!) upon which they have been hung to dry. Ganymede, a Siren, and Aurora are engaged in mutual civilities; the Eagle is feeding her baby; the Witch is cutting a cat's tail to get blood for scenic purposes, and two little devils—"their foreheads budding with their first horns"—are fighting at an altar for a pot of beer. The plate is crowded with minute strokes of humour—as the fowls roosting upon the waves, the "jewels" in a hamper, the kittens sporting with the orb, the plays in the bishop's mitre; but the mere catalogue of them would be lengthy. The worst fault of the design is that it has no central interest, although we may agree with Walpole that "for wit and imagination *without any other end*" (the italics are ours) it is "the best of all his works."

In the establishment of the Foundling Hospital, for which a Royal Charter was granted in 1739, Hogarth seems to have taken a genuine interest. From the first we find him associating himself with the patient benevolence of Captain Thomas Coram, who had grown grey in the praiseworthy enterprise to which, seventeen years before, he had been incited by the miserable condition of deserted children. These, in the then state of the Poor Laws, were consigned to the casual humanity of the passer-by. In the Hospital Charter Hogarth appears as a "Governor and Guardian," he was an active member at its meetings, and he aided it with his money, his graver, and his brush. The little print called *The Foundlings*, 1739, was intended as a "head-piece" to a power of attorney drawn up for the use of the establishment; its arms were designed by him; he painted an admirable portrait of its founder, and one of its vice-presidents, Martin Folkes, a mathematician and antiquarian of celebrity; and, lastly, with him originated that famous proposal to ornament the building with pictures, which ultimately "made a visit to the Foundling the most fashionable morning lounge of the reign of George II.," to say nothing of the fact that to this exhibition of paintings by native artists is to be traced, in all probability, the germ of our present Royal Academy.

Hogarth considered *Captain Coram* the best of his single portraits, and posterity has ratified his opinion. "The portrait which I painted with most pleasure (says he), and in which I particularly wished to excel, was that of Captain Coram, for the Foundling Hospital; and if I am so wretched an artist as my enemies assert, it is somewhat strange that this, which was one of the first I painted the size of life, should stand the test of twenty years' competition, and be generally thought the best portrait in the place, notwithstanding the first painters in the kingdom exerted all their talents to vie with it." The rivals referred to were Shackleton, Hudson, Reynolds (then plain Mr.), Cotes, Ramsay (the poet's son), Highmore, and Wilson. But the great genius of Sir Joshua had not attained its majority in that portrait of *Lord Dartmouth*, to which reference is made, and it must certainly be admitted that the picture of Coram stands a successful comparison with any of the remaining portraits in the Foundling.

To return to the succession of prints. In 1738 Hogarth issued eight plates to Jarvis's quarto translation of "Don Quixote." Like the rest of his illustrations to books they have no especial value. The hard frost of 1739-40, which stimulated so many delineators of "Ice-Fairs" and the like, appears to have passed by him unnoticed. But to the years 1740 and 1741 belong two delightful single plates, the *Distrest Poet*, and the *Enraged Musician*. The former of these had indeed been issued as far back as 1736, but it was republished with certain variations in 1740, and was followed a year after by the **Enraged Musician**, with which it is convenient to treat it. From a letter published by Ireland, and an advertisement in the "London Daily Post," for Nov. 24th, 1740, the artist appears to have contemplated a "**third on Painting**," but although there is reason to believe that a sketch in oils was completed, for some unexplained reason it was never engraved.

Was Goldsmith thinking of the *Distrest Poet* when, in August, 1758, he described himself as "in a garret, writing for bread, and expecting to be dunned for a milk-score?" Except that the milkmaid has already arrived, and is angrily exhibiting her tally, this is the precise *status quo* of Hogarth's print. The poor verseman, high in his Grub-Street or "Porridge-Island" sky-parlour, has risen by candlelight to finish a poem on "Riches" for some contemporary Curll. He is exactly in the case of Cowper's bard—

> "Who having whelp'd a prologue with much pains,
> Feels himself spent, and fumbles for his brains."

Neither the map of the "Gold Mines of Peru" upon his walls, nor Bysshe's "Art of Poetry," nor "all his books around," a magnificent total of three (we are describing the impression of 1740[1]), can help him at his need. Mean-

---

[1] The impression of Mar. 3, 1736, has under it the four following lines from Pope (adapted):—

> "Studious he sate, with all his books around,
> Sinking from thought to thought, a vast profund !

while his vociferous creditor (with the Michaelmas daisies round her hat) clamours for the score; the awakened child is crying, and the wind whistles "through the broken pane." He has a consolation, however, that poor Goldsmith lacked through life, one of the sweetest female companions that Hogarth ever drew. She is the ancestress of Thackeray's "Mrs. Shandon," this patient **conciliatory** lady. And (O bathos! O "most lame and **impotent** conclusion!") she is repairing her husband's small clothes, while the cat and kittens nestle cosily upon his worship's coat.

The *Enraged Musician* is more crowded with incident; but not nearly so suggestive. It is simply an apotheosis of discord. Cats wrangle on the tiles, a dog howls dismally, bells ring in the steeple, and a sweep shrills from a chimney-pot. Below a dustman bawls "Dust-Ho!" a costermonger yells "Flound-a-a-rs!" **and** a knife-grinder, a ballad-woman singing **the** "Lady's Fall," **an** oboe-player, **an** amateur drummer, **and an escaped** parrot swell the orchestra. And all this **cacophony for the** benefit of the befrogged (and, of course, **foreign**) violinist, who glares, infuriate, from his open window! The picture, in truth, as Fielding said, is deafening to look at.

Besides this pair of prints, the only other work of this period (a moderately successful portrait of *Bishop Hoadly* excepted) which need be chronicled, is the painting called *Taste in High Life*. It was not a favourite with Hogarth;

Plung'd for his sense, but found no bottom there;
Then writ, and flounder'd on, in mere despair."

Dunciad, book i.

Instead of **a poem on "Riches,"** he is writing on "Poverty," and instead of **the "Mines of Peru" there is** a print of Pope thrashing Curll. There **are also two more books.**

but affords a capital idea of the extremes of fashionable foible in 1742.

In the year 1745 (we are straying a few months beyond the limits of our chapter) Hogarth advertised several of his pictures for sale by a kind of auction. As usual, his method was entirely characteristic and original.

"The biddings [we quote from Nichols] were to remain open from the first to the last day of *February*, on these conditions: '1. That every bidder shall have an entire leaf numbered in the book of sale, on the top of which will be entered the name and place of abode, the sum paid by him, the time when, and for which picture. 2. That, on last day of sale, a clock (striking every five minutes) shall be placed in the room; and when it hath struck five minutes after twelve, the first picture mentioned in the sale-book will be deemed as sold; the second picture when the clock hath struck the next five minutes after twelve; and so on successively till the whole nineteen pictures are sold. 3. That none advance less than gold at each bidding. 4. No person to bid on the last day, except those whose names were before entered in the book. As Mr. *Hogarth's* room is but small, he begs the favour that no persons, except those whose names are entered in the book, will come to view his paintings on the last day of sale.' The pictures were sold for the following prices:—

	£	s.	d.
Six *Harlot's Progress*, at 14 guineas each	88	4	0
Eight *Rake's Progress*, at 22 guineas each	184	16	0
Morning, 20 guineas	21	0	0
Noon, 37 guineas	38	17	0
Evening, 38 guineas	39	18	0
Night, 26 guineas	27	6	0
Strolling Players, 26 guineas	27	6	0
	£427	7	0"

The ticket of admission was the etching known as the *Battle of the Pictures*, an idea probably suggested by Swift's "Battle of the Books;" and which depicts a spirited engagement between the **canvases** of the Black Masters on the one hand, and those **of Hogarth on the** other. Even in the inscription upon this ticket there is a touch of that half-ironic, **half-defiant** tone, **which is never** absent from the painter's public announcements:—"*The Bearer hereof is Entitled* (if he thinks **proper**) *to be a Bidder for* Mr. Hogarth's Pictures, *which are to be sold on the Last day of this Month.*" The prices realized were of course wholly inadequate; **but it must, we** fear, be remembered that the method of **sale was peculiar,** and little calculated to attract or conciliate the limited public of purchasers.

CHAPTER V.

THE MARRIAGE-À-LA-MODE.

1745.

THE auction with which the last chapter concluded took place in February, 1745; and the six paintings of *Marriage-à-la-Mode* were announced for sale,— "as soon as the Plates then taking from them should be completed." A hint of the series had already been given in the *Battle of the Pictures*, where a copy of the second scene is viciously assailed by a copy of the *Aldobrandini Marriage*. In April, 1745, the set of engravings was issued;—Plates i. and vi. being engraved by Scotin, Plates ii. and iii. by Baron, and Plates iv. and v. by Ravenet. Exactly two years before Hogarth had heralded them by the following notification in the "London Daily Post, and General Advertiser," of April 2nd, 1743:—"Mr. HOGARTH intends to publish by Subscription, SIX PRINTS from Copper-Plates, engrav'd by the best Masters in Paris, after his own Paintings; representing a Variety of *Modern Occurrences* in *High-Life*, and called MARRIAGE-A-LA-MODE. Particular care will be taken, that there may not be the least Objection to the Decency or Elegancy of the whole Work, and that none of the Characters represented shall be personal."[1] Then follow the terms of subscription. The last quoted lines were probably a bark at some forgotten detraction; and, if not actually ironical, doubtless about as sincere as Fielding's promise, in the prologue to his first comedy, not to offend the ladies. Those who had found indecency and inelegancy in the previous productions of the painter, would still see the same defects in the master-piece he now submitted to the public. And although it may be said that the "characters" represented are not "personal" in a satirical sense, more than one of them have been confidently identified with well-known originals. It would be almost impossible that they should not be. Like Molière, Hogarth took his material where he found it. It lay about him in the daily occurrences of his time; and unconsciously as well as consciously, real actors found their way into his "comedies with the pencil." As a matter of course, they were not absent from *Marriage-à-la-Mode*.

How "well-preserved," even in this year of grace 1879, these wonderful pictures are! It would seem as if Time, in mistaken malice, had resolved to ignore in every way the courageous little artist who treated him with such frequent indignity. Look at them in the National Gallery. Look, too, at the cracks and fissures in the Wilkies —the soiled rainbows of Turner—the bituminous riding-habit of Lady Douro in Sir Edwin's "Story of Waterloo." But these paintings of William Hogarth, which, when fresh from the easel, found their timid purchaser in Mr.

---

[1] To the advertisement of April 4 and subsequent issues was added:— "The Heads for the better Preservation of the Characters and Expressions to be done by the Author."

Lane of Hillingdon, are fresh to-day. They are not worked like a Denner, it is true, and the artist is sometimes less solicitous about his method than the result of it; yet they are soundly, straightforwardly, and skilfully painted. Lady Bingley's red hair, Carestini's nostril, are shown in the simplest and directest manner. But everywhere the desired effect **is exactly** produced, and **without** effort. Take, for example, **the** inkstand in the **first scene, with** its sand-box and bell. In these days it **would be a patient** *trompe-l'œil*, probably better **done than** the figures using it. Here it is sufficiently **indicated,** though not elaborated ; it **holds its exact** place **as a** piece of furniture, **and nothing more.** And at this point it should be added **that if in** the ensuing descriptions we should speak of **colour,** our readers will know that we are describing not the engravings of Messrs. Scotin and the rest, but Hogarth's **own** pictures at Trafalgar Square. It is the **more** necessary to say this, because the paintings frequently differ slightly from the engravings.

The **first** picture of the series represents the *Marriage Contract*. The **scene, as** the artist is careful to signify by the **liberal coronets on** the furniture and accessories, is laid **in the house of an** earl, who, with his gouty foot swathed **in bandages, seems** with a superb (if somewhat stiff-jointed) dignity **to** be addressing certain observations respecting himself and his pedigree to a sober-looking personage opposite, who, spectacles on nose, is peering at the endorsement of the " Marriage Settel^{mt} of the R^t Honble Lord Viscount Squanderfield." This figure, which **is that** of a London merchant, **by its** turned-in toes, the **point of** the sword-sheath between **the legs,** and the awkward constraint of its attitude forms **an** admirable contrast to the other. A massive gold chain shows the wearer to be an alderman. Between the two is a third person, probably the merchant's confidential clerk or cashier, who holds out a "Mortgage" to the earl. Gold and notes lie upon the table, where also are an inkstand, sealing-wax, and a lighted candle in which a "thief" is conspicuous. At the back of this trio is the affianced couple—the earl's son and the alderman's daughter. It is in fact an alliance of *sacs et parchemins*, in which the young people are rather involved than interested. The lady, who is fresh and pretty in her bridal-dress, wears a mingled expression of *mauvaise honte* and distaste for her position, and trifles with the ring, which she has strung upon her handkerchief, while a brisk and well-built young lawyer, who trims a pen, bends towards her with a whispered compliment. Meantime the viscount, a frail, effeminate-looking figure, with an open snuff-box, turns away from her in fatuous foppery towards a pier-glass at his side. His coat is light-blue, his vest is loaded with embroidery, he wears an enormous *solitaire*, and has red-heels to his shoes. Before him (in happy parody of the ill-matched pair) are two dogs in coupling-links:—the bitch sits up, alert and curious, her companion is lying down. The only other figure is that of an old lawyer, who, with a plan in his hand, and a gesture of contemptuous wonder, looks through an open window at an unfinished and ill-designed building, in front of which several idle servants are lounging or sitting.

The pictures on the wall exhibit and satirize the taste of the time. The largest is a portrait in the French style of one of the earl's ancestors, who traverses the canvas victoriously. A cannon explodes below him, a comet is

seen above; and, in his right hand, notwithstanding his cuirass and voluminous Queen Anne peruke, he wields the lightning of Jupiter. *Judith and Holofernes, St. Sebastian, The Murder of Abel, David and Goliath, The Martyrdom of St. Laurence,* are some of the rest, all of which, it will be seen, belong to those " dismal dark subjects, neither entertaining nor ornamental," against which we have already heard the painter inveigh. Upon the ceiling is *Pharaoh in the Red Sea.* A Gorgon in a sconce appears to be surveying the transaction with horror. Hogarth has used a similar idea in the *Strollers,* where the same face seems astounded at the airy freedom of the light-clad lady who there takes the part of Diana.

In the picture of the *Contract,* the young couple and "Connsellor Silvertongue," as he has been christened, are placed in close proximity. These are the real actors of the drama. The old earl is seen no more henceforth; the alderman appears only at the end of the story. The next scene is laid in a handsome saloon.[1] A clock shows the time to be twenty minutes after one; but lights are still smouldering in the chandelier; and a yawning footman in curl-papers is languidly arranging the furniture in the background. From the cards and "Hoyle" on the floor, the two violins and the music-book, it must be inferred that the establishment is only now awaking from the fatigues of a prolonged entertainment. At a round table by the fire, with a teapot and one cup upon it, sits the lady of the house, who, in a coquettish night-cap and morning jacket, stretches her arms wearily, with a

---

[1] This room, we have been given to understand, was copied from the drawing-room of a house in Arlington Street.

sidelong glance at her husband, who reclines upon, or rather is supported by, a chair at the opposite side of the fireplace. Nothing in Hogarth is finer than this latter figure. Worn out and nauseated, he has returned from some independent debauch. His rich black velvet coat and his waistcoat are thrown open, his disordered hair has lost its ribbon, his hands are thrust deeply into his small-clothes. He still wears his hat. His sword, which lies upon the floor, is broken; and a lap-dog snuffs at a woman's cap, half thrust into his pocket. His whole appearance—the lassitude of his posture, the tired and cynical disgust upon his features—all manifest the reaction after excess in an already enfeebled constitution. Hazlitt, in his review of these pictures at the Exhibition of 1814, pointed out how skilfully his pallid face is contrasted with the yellow-whitish colour of the mantelpiece behind. He seems in a stupor; and neither he nor his wife takes any notice of the Methodist steward, who, after a vain attempt to attract attention to his accounts, quits the room with uplifted eyes and *one* paid bill on his file. A book labelled "Regeneration" peeps from his pocket. This is the only other figure in the picture.

The room in which this scene takes place is another vivid illustration of the interiors of the Georgian era. It is divided into two by an arch supported on dark blue marble pillars. The pictures visible on the walls (one of which is partially veiled by a curtain, and reveals only a naked human foot) are less striking than those in Pl. i. Indeed, those in the background appear to be figures of the Apostles. Over the mantelpiece in front is Cupid playing upon the bagpipes in a ruined landscape; immediately below him is a bust with mended nose, which Lichtenberg conjectures to represent "Faustina." On either side the shelf is crowded with oriental monstrosities—toads and the "fat squabs"—so well described in Cowper's couplet:—

> " Gorgonius sits, abdominous and **wan**,
> Like a fat squab upon a **Chinese fan**."

On the right hand of the **mantelpiece hangs a nondescript trophy** of leafage **in brass surrounding a clock, and surmounted by a cat in china, life size. Below this, fishes** appear among the **leaves. The whole, like the bad architecture** in Pl. i., **is probably a further satire on** William Kent, who designed **everything, from** picture-frames to petticoats.

It is evident that the viscount and his lady have elected to **take** their pleasures apart. What those pleasures are we are shown more specifically in the third and fourth pictures. Over that relating to those **of the** husband, we shall not linger long, both by reason of its subject and the obscurity of its story. None of the commentators—not even those whose inspiration is said **to be** derived from Hogarth himself—have given a satisfactory **explanation** of it. Churchill, in the after-days of his enmity, **affirmed that the** artist himself did not know, but had **worked from the** imperfectly apprehended suggestion **of some** friend. **This, in a man of** Hogarth's type, is not **probable. It is more likely that** he did not choose to be quite explicit. **The design may** be thus briefly described. The reader will remember a woman's cap (in the painting it has a *blue* ribbon) which peeped from the viscount's pocket in the saloon scene. In this picture, a similar blue-ribboned cap is worn by a slight girlish figure in a laced " manteel " and brocaded gown, who has been apparently brought by the nobleman to consult a quack doctor. Her health, and his treatment of it, **is** certainly the question in debate; and the viscount, who is seated, with lifted cane threatens a fierce-looking and masculine woman (who may be the quack's wife, or a procuress, or both), to whom he sarcastically holds out a box of pills. She, in return, is preparing to retort with a clasp knife. The bow-legged quack, an admirable figure, whose face, Hazlitt says happily, "seems as if it were composed of salve," stands near her; and is apparently addressing some snarling query to the unfortunate patient, who listens in a mute, impassive posture, with a handkerchief to her mouth. But if the meaning of the figures is not clear, there is no doubt about their surroundings. They are the stock-in-trade of an empiric of the first water. Skulls, stuffed alligators, retorts, mummies, and the like, decorate the apartment. To the left of the picture is a cumbrous apparatus of levers and cog-wheels for setting collar-bones; near this is a smaller one devoted to the humbler office of drawing corks. Both are invented by "Mons. de la Pillule" (presumably the quack himself), and have been "seen and approved by the Royal Academy of Sciences at Paris." The room, according to Nollekens, was copied from one in 96, St. Martin's Lane, once the residence of Dr. Misaubin, the lean doctor of the *Harlot's Progress*, Pl. v., who died there in April, 1734. He was the proprietor of a famous pill; and if, as Nollekens further says, he had an "Irish wife," it may well be that Hogarth, though he did not reproduce the actual individuals, was really thinking of the Misaubin *ménage*.[1]

---

[1] Much material for suggestion respecting the meaning of this picture is contained in Mr. F. G. Stephens' "Catalogue" under *Prenez des Pilules*, No. 1,987; *Quackery Unmask'd, Or, Empiricism display'd*, No. 3,019; and in the account of Pl. v. of *A Harlot's Progress*.

In the next picture (the *Toilet Scene*) we pass to the bedroom of the countess, a lofty chamber, with the great bed, after the eighteenth century fashion, standing in its alcove, and surmounted by **a coronet**. There **is** another over the mirror; the old earl is certainly dead. **The pictures** on the wall are *Jupiter and Io*, *Lot and his Daughters*, **the** *Rape of Ganymede*, and the portrait of . . *Counsellor Silvertongue!* That gentleman himself,

"*Gros et gras,* **le teint frais,** *et la bouche vermeille,*"

(like Molière's **"Tartuffe"**), **is** reclining easily upon a sofa, and talking **with** facile familiarity to the countess, who sits **at her toilet** table in a *peignoir* and yellow dressing gown, under the hands of a Swiss valet, who is curling her hair. That she is now a mother **is** shown by **the** child's coral hanging from her chair. She listens with a pleased expression to her admirer's conversation, which, from his indication of the figures on the screen at **his** back, and **the** masquerade ticket in his hand, appears to refer to that entertainment; but we fail to find in her **look** "the heightened **glow, the** forward intelligence, and loosened soul **of** love," which Hazlitt found **in it**. It is possible to **be even too sympathetic as a critic.**

These two are absorbed in their **own affairs.** The **rest** of the **company,** with exception of **one** stout gentleman in the background, who is asleep, are listening intently to the performances of an Italian singer and a German flute-player. Into the portrait of the former (said to represent the famous counter-tenor Carestini) Hogarth has **infused** all his spleen against exotic artists. The huge, awkward form, the gross, almost swinish, physiognomy, the pampered look and posture, the profusion of jewels, and the splendid costume of the popular idol are all expressed with the closest fidelity. The flute-player is a certain Weideman. The chief listener is a red-haired lady in a cottage hat and white dress, Mrs. Fox Lane, afterwards Lady Bingley, to whom is attributed the notorious saying, "One God, one Farinelli." She sways herself to the notes in an ecstasy, oblivious of her black boy, who hands her some chocolate, and is amazed at his mistress's enthusiasm. Sitting near her, a gentleman, with a fan hanging from his wrist, screws his face into an affected simper of delight; and next to him, a slim macaroni, with his hair in curl papers, and his *queue* loose like a woman's tresses, sips at his cup with a fixed look of resigned connoisseurship. Both are fantastic and ridiculous: what other men (according to Hogarth) would listen, or pretend to listen, to Italian singers? The foreground is littered with invitation and other cards, while in the right-hand corner is a pile of recent purchases from an auction (perhaps Mr. Cock's in the Piazza). A second black boy, who kneels beside them, significantly touches the horns of an Actæon.

The next pictures pass swiftly to the tragic termination of the story. The fifth scene, as appears from the paper on the floor, is laid in the "Turk's Head Bagnio." Upon the counsellor and the countess, who have repaired to this place after the masquerade, the earl has come suddenly, bursting open the lock, of which the hasp lies upon the ground. A table has been hastily thrust aside, a stool with its litter of female apparel overturned, and the quarrel between the husband and the seducer has been fought out briefly and fatally in the dying firelight. The counsellor, naked, escapes by the window; the earl, run through the body, totters with filmy eyes and falling

Page 56.

sword in the centre of the room. His wife, agonized with terror and remorse, has flung herself on her knees at his feet, while the frightened host, a constable, and a watchman are entering at the door.

The last scene shows the old home in the city, to which, in her dishonour, the countess has returned. Through the window we see London Bridge with the tottering houses upon it which were taken down in 1758. "Counsellor Silvertongue" has been hung for murder, his "Last Dying Speech" is on the floor. The countess has poisoned herself with laudanum fetched by a half-witted servant, and a whimpering old woman holds up a rickety child to kiss its dying mother.[1] Meanwhile the doctor pompously quits the apartment, the apothecary rudely rates the imbecile messenger, and the alderman with prudent forethought draws off a valuable ring from his daughter's finger.

We have dealt briefly with these concluding pictures. Yet the decorations and accessories are to the full as minute and effective as those of the ones which precede them. The furniture of the bagnio, with its portrait of *Moll Flanders*, humorously continued by the sturdy legs of a soldier in the mouldy *Judgment of Solomon* behind, the candle flaring in the draught of the open door and window, the reflection of the lantern on the ceiling and the tongs on the floor, the horror-stricken look on the mask of the lady and the satanic grin on that of her paramour, all deserve notice. So do the gross Dutch pictures in the alderman's

---

[1] Mr. Sala, in an interesting paper in the "Gentleman's Magazine" on George Cruikshank, notes that the poor child is a girl. The earl is the last of his race in the male line, and the title is extinct. This is one of those wonderful touches which, except in Hogarth, we may vainly seek for.

house, the pewter plates and the silver goblet, the stained table-cloth, the egg in rice, and the pig's head which the ravenous dog is stealing. There is no defect of invention, no superfluity of detail, no purposeless stroke in this "owre true tale." From first to last it progresses steadily to its catastrophe by a gradual march of skilfully linked and developed incidents. It is like a novel of Fielding on canvas ; and it seems almost inconceivable that, with this magnificent work *en évidence* (for it was not sold till some years after it was painted, and was exhibited freely both at the "Golden Head" and Cock's Auction Rooms), the critics of that age should have been contented to re-echo the after-opinion of Walpole that "as a painter Hogarth had but slender merit," and to cackle the foot-rule criticisms of the Rev. Mr. Gilpin as to his ignorance of composition. But so it was. Not until that exhibition of his works at the British Institution in 1814, to which reference has been made, was it thoroughly understood how excellent and original both as a designer and a colourist was this native artist, whom "picture-dealers, picture-cleaners, picture-frame makers, and other connoisseurs,"— to use his own ironical words,—had been allowed to rank below the third-rate copyists of third-rate foreigners.

In the year 1750 the set of paintings passed to a Mr. Lane of Hillingdon, near Uxbridge, by one of those unfortunate auctions devised by Hogarth for disposing of his works. The bidding was to be by written tickets, and the highest bidder at noon on the 6th of June was to be the purchaser. Picture-dealers were by the scheme expressly excluded as bidders. Whether this mode of sale, announced as usual by a characteristic notice in the "Daily Advertiser," " disobliged the Town " or not, it is certain that when Mr. Lane arrived at the "Golden Head," he was the only bidder who had put in an appearance.[1] The highest offer having been declared to be £120, Mr. Lane shortly before twelve said he would "make the **pounds guineas**," but subsequently, and much to his credit, **offered the artist a delay of some hours to** find a better purchaser. **An** hour passed, and **as no one** had appeared Hogarth surrendered the pictures to **Mr. Lane,** who thus for £126 became the fortunate **possessor of the** *Marriage-à-la-Mode,* in Carlo Maratti frames which **had cost four guineas a-piece**! In 1797 **they were purchased at** Christie's by Mr. Angerstein for **£1,381, and passed,** with his collection, to their present **home in the** National Gallery.

In **1746** a description of the prints in Hudibrastic verse was published, under the title of "Marriage-à-la-Mode; an Humourous Tale in Six Cantos," &c. It has no especial value. Shebbeare's novel of "The Marriage Act," and Colman and Garrick's farce of "The Clandestine Marriage," **are** also said to have been prompted by this series. Hogarth himself **projected a** companion *Happy Marriage,* **some designs for** which have been preserved. **The idea was however abandoned, not,** as Wilkes obligingly informs

---

[1] Not the "**sole** bidder," as Allan Cunningham and others have inferred. If this were **so,** in "making the pounds guineas," Mr. Lane would be bidding against himself, a thing which sometimes occurs at auctions, but is not recommended. We have failed to find any other account of this transaction than that supplied to Nichols for his second edition of 1782 by Mr. Lane himself, and which is summarized above. Cunningham seems to have derived his information from the same source; **but he** strangely transforms it. We can but surmise that he followed **Ireland's** transcript, in which the highest bid is given at £110 instead of £120—a rather unfortunate mistake, **for it** appears to have misled a good many people.

us, because "the rancour and malevolence" of the artist's mind "made him very soon turn with envy and disgust from objects of so pleasing contemplation"; but no doubt because the placid features of contented matrimony did not afford the needful variety to his pencil. As to Major's suggestion, with which we may close this chapter, that there is a relationship between the *Marriage-à-la-Mode* and Dryden's play of the same name, we have only to say, after reading the latter, that it appears to have no greater weight than Fluellen's comparison of Macedon with Monmouth. There is a husband and wife in the one, and a husband and wife in the other, and there are seducers in both.

CHAPTER VI.

CONTEMPORARIES.   MARCH TO FINCHLEY.   MINOR PRINTS.

1746 to 1752.

IN the narrative of Hogarth's life nothing is more tantalizing than the absence of gossip respecting his contemporaries and friends. His social qualities and the popularity of his prints (for notwithstanding the poor prices he received for his pictures his prints were now widely circulated), should, one would think, have brought him into frequent contact with many of the eminent or notorious personages of his time. At places like "Old Slaughter's Coffee-House" in St. Martin's Lane or "The Feathers" in Leicester Fields, at the "Turk's Head" in Gerard Street and the annual dinner at the Foundling Hospital, at the "Beef-Steak Club" or in the green-rooms of Drury-Lane and Covent Garden, he must have met most of the existing or future artistic and literary celebrities. But the record of such encounters is, in the main, conspicuous for its absence. We are aware, indeed, that he was familiar with the Hoadly family. He painted the bishop, as we have stated, and he left a scene from Benjamin Hoadly's "Suspicious Husband;" whilst, on the other hand, Dr. John Hoadly supplied him with the verses for the *Rake's*

Progress. He knew Dr. Morell, Mr. Townley, Dr. Arnold King, Fielding's friend Ralph—the Ralph of "The Champion" and "The Dunciad"—and Ireland prints a letter to him from the great Bishop Warburton. Walpole timidly patronized him, and invited him to a dinner with Gray the poet, which, if we may believe George Steevens, does not appear to have been a success. He visited Richardson in Salisbury Court. Here he made the acquaintance of Dr. Johnson, of his first meeting with whom there is a comical account in Boswell; and he was on terms of great familiarity with Mrs. Piozzi, then Miss Salusbury, who calls him her "dear Mr. Hogarth," and refers to the "odd particular directions about dress, dancing, and many other matters" that he used to give her as a girl. In his last years he had some intercourse with Goldsmith, and, according to Mr. Forster, made a sketch of him hard at work in his Islington lodgings, not forgetting the ruffles and rings in which poor "Goldy" delighted. He was at one time intimate with Wilkes and Churchill (although but for his unfortunate quarrel with them we might never have heard of that fact), and had been the guest of Sir Francis Dashwood (Lord Despencer), whom he painted in his Medmenham Abbey costume. But the friendship of which we find most certain traces is that with Fielding and Garrick. As we have seen, Fielding had written of him admiringly in the "Champion" and "Joseph Andrews," and refers to his prints for the prototypes of more than one of his characters. Hogarth, on his side, etched benefit tickets for Fielding, and we shall find him in this chapter assisting him with a head-piece for one of his numerous literary ventures. With Garrick his connection probably began not long after the great actor's first appearance at Good-

man's Fields in 1741, and it continued until his (Hogarth's) death. One of the most charming of the letters in the "Garrick Correspondence" is a graceful apology to the painter for remissness in visiting him: and later, when Churchill had announced that he was meditating his unjustifiable "Epistle," Garrick took care to expostulate:—
"I must intreat of you" (says an autograph note in the Forster Collection) "by the Regard you profess to me, that you don't tilt at my Friend Hogarth before you see me. . . . . He is a great and original Genius, I love him as a Man and reverence him as an Artist. I would not for all the Politicks and Politicians in the universe that you two should have the least cause of Ill-will to each other. I am sure you will not publish against him if you think twice." Unhappily Churchill was not to be so controlled. But this extract pleasantly illustrates the relations of Hogarth and "Little Davy," of whom he left several portraits, the most important of which, the *Garrick as Richard III.*, was engraved in 1746—the year with which this chapter opens.

"For the portrait of Mr. Garrick in Richard III.," says Hogarth, "I was paid two hundred pounds (which was more than any English artist ever received for a single portrait), and that too by the sanction of several painters who had previously been consulted about the price, which was not given without mature consideration." The purchaser was Mr. Duncombe, of Duncombe Park, Yorkshire; and, in truth, when one remembers that the *Marriage-à-la-Mode* only fetched £126, it must be admitted that the price paid for the *Garrick* was munificent. The picture itself, which, with *Sigismonda*, was exhibited at the British Institution in 1856, is striking and effective, but unless much is allowed for the exaggeration of acting, the resemblance to Garrick's face and figure is not great. Hogarth has left a better likeness in the bright little picture of *Garrick and his Wife*, which belonged to the late Mr. Locker of Greenwich Hospital, who sold it to George IV. Here the actor is represented in the act of writing the prologue to Foote's comedy of "Taste," while his wife behind him takes the pen from his hand, a conceit which —as Steevens is careful to acquaint us—is borrowed from Vanloo's portrait of *Colley Cibber and his Daughter*. This work appears to have suffered the unaccountable fate of some other of the artist's efforts. A dispute arose between Garrick and Hogarth on the subject; and the latter in a fit of spleen drew his brush across the face. The picture remained unpaid for at his death, when his widow sent it to Garrick without any demand. Another likeness of Garrick is contained in the frontispiece to the "Farmer's Return," an interlude by him which was very popular in 1762, where an honest farmer pays a visit to the "fine hugeous city" of London, witnesses the coronation of George III., goes to see Laureate Whitehead's "School for Lovers," and sits up with the "Cock Lane Ghost." Finally to complete the sum of Hogarth's relations with the "English Roscius," he designed him a chair at the time of the Shakespeare Jubilee, for which he carved a medallion from a piece of the Stratford mulberry tree.[1]

But in the August of 1746 Hogarth produced a portrait in which his characteristic powers are far more evident than in any picture he ever made of Garrick. In that month

---

[1] There is now (1879) a portrait of Mrs. Garrick by Hogarth in the South Kensington Museum. It is lent by the Earl of Dunmore.

the notorious Simon Fraser, Lord Lovat, was brought in a litter to St. Albans on his way to London, where he was tried, and subsequently executed on Tower Hill. Hogarth, upon the invitation of a local physician (Samuel Ireland's friend Dr. Webster) travelled to St. Albans to meet him. He found him on the 14th at the "White Hart" in the hands of a barber. The old lord (he was over seventy) rose at his approach, embracing him after the French fashion on the cheek, and, says the chronicle, transferring some of the soapsuds on his face to that of the painter. The short squat figure, the watchful attitude, and the "pawky" expression of Lovat as he counts the Clans on his fingers, are admirably rendered. It is no wonder that this effective sketch, having besides its own merit all that of an *àpropos*, should have been widely popular. The rolling press could not supply impressions enough; and though they were sold at a shilling each, for several weeks Hogarth received payment at the rate of twelve pounds a day.

To the following year belong *The Stage Coach; or, Country Inn Yard*, and the series called *Industry and Idleness*. The former is more interesting as a little piece of every-day English eighteenth century life than for any dramatic element which it contains, although there is an election procession in the background. From the wooden-galleried courtyard of the *Old Angel Inn*, Tom Bates from London, the creaking and lumbering Ilford stage (?) prepares to run its snail-like course of so many miles *per diem*. "T. B." himself may be seen in the foreground, justifying his lengthy score to a hard-featured lawyer (with the "Act against Bribery" in his pocket), who discharges it unwillingly. Mrs. Landlady, from her *sanctum* among the strong waters, is bawling for Susan Chambermaid, who is detained by the farewells of a gentleman in a bag-wig. A stout woman is being squeezed in at the coach-door by a man, who hands a dram-bottle after her. Behind come a vinegar-faced spinster in a Joseph and hood, and a squalling child. To the right, a portly personage, with a sword and cane, disregarding an appeal from the hunchbacked postilion, prepares to follow the stout woman. In the "basket" an old crone is smoking among the baggage; and, on the roof, an English sailor (see "Centurion" on the bundle) and a dejected Frenchman have taken their perilous places. To put the finishing touch to the bustle of departure, a man blows a post-horn out of a window. The whole scene might serve as an illustration to "Peregrine Pickle" or "Tom Jones."

Industry and Idleness, says Hogarth himself, exhibited "the conduct of two fellow 'prentices: where the one by taking good courses, and pursuing points for which he was put apprentice, becomes a valuable man, and an ornament to his country: the other, by giving way to idleness, naturally falls into poverty, and ends fatally, as is expressed in the last print." The end, as Leigh Hunt says, was "an avowed commonplace," . . . "while the execution of it was full of much higher things and profounder humanities." There is no finer stroke in Hogarth than that by which the miserable player at "halfpenny-under-the-hat," in Pl. iii., is shown to have but a plank between him and the grave; nor is there anything more forcible in its squalid realism than the episode in Thomas Idle's career to which Dr. King subjoined the epigraph—"The sound of a shaken leaf shall chase him." Very piteous, too, is the grief of the widowed mother when her reprobate son is being sculled past Cuckold's **Point to the ship which is to carry his graceless fortunes to a foreign land.** The whole set of prints, **which we cannot further** describe, is full of contemporary detail **of the most interesting character.** In Pl. vi. we **see the newly married couple** fêted by the old discordant **hymenæan (a "kind of wild Janizary music,"** Lichtenberg **calls it) of the marrow-bone and cleaver men.**[1] **Pl. viii. shows a civic feast; and the two final plates** a Lord **Mayor's Show and an execution at Tyburn. The idea for this series is said to** have been suggested **by the " Eastward Hoe "** of Chapman, Jonson, and Marston, **with which it has some** affinities. Though coarsely **executed it was** very popular, was dramatized, and gave rise to several publications, graphic and otherwise. One of these was the imitation of Northcote, the history of two housemaids, patched together from Hogarth and Richardson's " Pamela." " There could not **be a** more lamentable failure," say the biographers of **Reynolds, " and Northcote never** forgave Hogarth."

In 1747 Hogarth executed **a rude** headpiece for the " **Jacobite's Journal,"** a newspaper begun by Henry Fielding in **the December of** that year, and having for its object the ridicule of Jacobite principles. Hogarth's **contribution** to it (if **indeed it be his)** does not require any **further** notice. In **the next year took** place **that memorable** journey to France **the narrative** of **which has afforded** so much delight to the more malicious **of his** biographers. **At** this date we may be content with his own version of

---

[1] " **When**, therefore, properly struck," says Lichtenberg of these instruments, " they produce no despicable clang ; at least certainly a better **one** than logs of wood emit when thrown to the ground ; and yet the latter are said **to** have occasioned the invention of the rebeck."

the story, without encumbering it with any of the variations of the commentators, amiable or otherwise. "The next print," says he, "I engraved was the *Roast Beef of Old England* [published March 6, 1749], which took its rise from a visit I paid to France the preceding year. The first time an Englishman goes from *Dover* to *Calais*, he must be struck with the different face of things at so little a distance. A farcical pomp of war, pompous parade of religion, and much bustle with very little business. To sum up all, poverty, slavery, and innate insolence, covered with an affectation of politeness, give you even here a true picture of the manners of the whole nation: nor are the priests less opposite to those of Dover, than the two shores. The friars are dirty, sleek, and solemn; the soldiery are lean, ragged, and tawdry; and as to the fish-women—their faces are absolute leather.

"As I was sauntering about and observing them, near the gate which it seems was built by the English, when the place was in our possession, I remarked some appearance of the arms of *England* on the front. By this and idle curiosity, I was prompted to make a sketch of it; which being observed, I was taken into custody; but not attempting to cancel any of my sketches or memorandums, which were found to be merely those of a painter for his private use, without any relation to fortification, it was not thought necessary to send me back to Paris.[1] I was only closely con-

---

[1] J. B. Nichols, who had an opportunity of consulting the original MSS. when in the possession of Mr. H. P. Standly, says that Ireland's transcripts of them are "most incorrectly copied." There is nothing in them about Paris, which is unfortunate for Ireland's note—"this proves he had reached Paris." J. B. Nichols' reference to the MSS. seems to have escaped the notice of the later commentators; but it throws grave doubts upon the accuracy of the Hogarth papers as printed by Ireland.

fined to my own lodgings, till the wind changed *for England:* where I no sooner arrived, than I set about the picture; made the gate my background; and in one corner introduced my own portrait, which has been generally thought a correct likeness, with the soldier's hand upon my shoulder. By the fat friar, who stops the lean cook that is sinking under the weight of a vast sirloin of beef, and two of *the military* bearing off a great kettle of *soup maigre,* I meant to display to my own countrymen the striking difference between the food, priests, soldiers, &c., of two nations so contiguous, that in a clear day one coast may be seen from the other. The melancholy and miserable Highlander, browzing on his scanty fare, consisting of a bit of bread and an onion, is intended for one of the many that fled from this country after the rebellion in 1744[5]." It is not necessary to add anything to this description of *Calais Gate,* save that Mr. Pine, the engraver, sat for the "fat friar," and that the painter's friend, Theodosius Forrest, made a cantata on the subject.[1] One of the French soldiers long served as a heading to recruiting advertisements.

The *Gate of Calais* was a subject which might well be expected to excite all the insular prejudices of Hogarth, to say nothing of the "least little touch of spleen" on his own account at the somewhat ignominious treatment he had received in France. But although he was so keenly alive to the "lean, ragged, and tawdry" appearance of the soldiers of the Grand Monarque he was not the less sensible of the weak points of the British Grenadier. In

---

[1] Nichols ("Genuine Works") calls him "Theophilus," but this is probably a slip of the pen. See note to Chap. ii., p. 17.

the *March of the Guards towards Scotland in the year* 1745, commonly called the *March to Finchley*, he has exhibited all the disorders of a military hegira. While the straggling vanguard are winding away to the horizon, the foreground, between the "King's Head" Inn and the "Adam and Eve" at Tottenham Court Turnpike, is filled with a confusion of departure that beggars all description. The most prominent figure is a young and handsome guardsman, hopelessly embarrassed by the rival adieux of two ladies, one violent, the other pathetic. Near him is a drummer who is endeavouring, with a comical screw of his face, to drown his own grief and that of his wife and child by a vigorous attack upon his drum. Elsewhere an officer kisses a milkmaid, while a soldier pours her milk into his hat; another soldier directs the attention of a grinning pieman to the episode, and takes the opportunity of abstracting his wares. A drunken fellow in the gutter turns disgustedly from a friendly offer of water and holds out his hand to a female sutler for more gin, while the shrivelled infant at her back imitates his gesture. The soft, unfurrowed face of another child in the crowd is happily contrasted with the plotting eagerness of a couple of Jacobite intriguers. In the background a fight is going on, watched by eager spectators. But here, as in so many other cases, we must resign ourselves to a mere indication of the chief riches of the plate. It has, however, been excellently described in the "Old Woman's Magazine," i. 182, and by Hogarth's and Fielding's friend, Mr. Justice Welch, in Christopher Smart's "Student," ii. 162. The artist at first intended to dedicate the picture to George II. That monarch had, as Walpole says, "little propensity to refined pleasures;" and he received it with anything but enthusiasm. It was ac-

cordingly dedicated to the King of Prussia as "an Encourager of *Arts* and *Sciences*," and his Majesty made a handsome acknowledgment of the honour done him. Like others of Hogarth's works, it was sold by lottery, and became the property of the Foundling Hospital, where it remains.

The print of the *March to Finchley* was published in December, 1750. The only other prints which concern this chapter are *Beer Street* and *Gin Lane*, 1751; the *Four Stages of Cruelty*, 1751; the two plates of *Paul before Felix*, 1751 and 1752, and *Moses brought to Pharaoh's Daughter*, 1752. The first pair, which seem to have been prompted by the agitation connected with the Act for restricting the sale of spirituous liquors, are among the best known of Hogarth's minor works, although Sir Wilfrid Lawson and the total abstainers would probably regard the bloated prosperity of *Beer Street* as scarcely less dangerous than the starved emaciation of *Gin Lane*. With the lusty beer-drinkers everything prospers but the pawnbroking business; with the consumers of "Bung-your-eye" and "Strip-me-naked" everything is the reverse, and the gentleman at the sign of the "three balls" is driving a roaring trade. We cannot linger on these plates further than to call attention to the inimitable professional complacency of the ragged sign-painter in *Beer Street* (in those days there was a regular sign-market in Harp Alley, Shoe Lane), and the terrible figure of the itinerant gin-seller and the maudlin mother in the companion print. Charles Lamb has left an enthusiastic description of this latter. The *Four Stages of Cruelty* are a set of plates exhibiting the "progress" of one Thomas Nero, who, from torturing dogs and horses, advances by rapid stages to seduction and murder, and finishes his career on the dissecting table at Surgeons' Hall. They have all the downright power of Hogarth's best manner; but they are unrelieved by humour of any kind, and consequently painful and even repulsive. "The leading points in these as well as in the two preceding prints," says Hogarth, "were made as obvious as possible, in the hope that their tendency might be seen by men of the lowest rank. Neither minute accuracy of design, nor fine engraving were deemed necessary, as the latter would render them too expensive for the persons to whom they were intended to be useful." These words should be borne in mind in considering them, especially the *Four Stages of Cruelty*. The price of the ordinary impressions was a shilling the plate, and an unsuccessful attempt was made to sell them even more cheaply by cutting them in wood.

Paul before Felix and *Moses brought to Pharaoh's Daughter* were essays in that historical style to which Hogarth now and then returned like the moth to the flame. The former was painted for Lincoln's Inn Hall, to decorate which Lord Wyndham had left a legacy of £200;[1] the latter the painter

---

[1] Hogarth obtained the commission through the instrumentality of Lord Mansfield. Recent search among the archives of the Society of Lincoln's Inn has brought to light the following letter and receipt with reference to this subject. We make no apology for inserting them here, especially as they have not hitherto been printed, and moreover establish the date of the painting:—

"June 28 1748

"S^r

"According to your order, I have consider'd of a place for the Picture, and cannot think of any better than that over the sound board, in the hall, all the advantages to be gain'd for Light, can only be by setting the bottom near the wall, and Inclining the Top forward as much as possible, it being thus Inclin'd will make ornaments on the sides improper, so that a Frame only is necessary. I have enquired of Mr Gosset a Frame maker in Barwick Street about the price of one some-

presented to the Foundling Hospital. Neither of them can be said to have been thoroughly successful, though Haydon certainly goes too far when he says that the painter merited a strait-waistcoat if he really thought the *Moses* a serious painting. But if they were not successful they were at all events the cause of a success. As a subscription ticket to the engravings of these two pictures Hogarth issued a burlesque *Paul before Felix*, "design'd and scratch'd in the true Dutch taste." Everything that he chose to see in Rembrandt and his school—the vulgarity—the want of beauty—the anachronisms in costume—is carefully ridiculed. This etching was at first merely given away to the artist's acquaintance, &c., but it became so popular that it sold for nearly as much as the larger prints. We

---

what in the manner of the Sketch below [*not printed*], he believes it may come to about 30 pound Guilt, to about half as much unguilt and about five pounds less if my Lord Windham's armes are omitted. Frames may be carried up to a great expense but he thinks one cannot be made in proportion to the picture for less.

"I am Sir your
"Most obed[t] Humble
"Ser[t] to com[d]
"W[m]. HOGARTH.

"I have removed the picture home again in hopes of making some improvements whilst the Frame is making."

"July the 8th 1748

"Rec[d] of Jn[o] Wood Esq[r] Treasurer of the Hon[ble] Society of Lincolns Inn by the hands of Rich[d] Farshall Chief Butler to the Said Society the Sum of two hundred pounds being the Legacy given by the late Lord Wyndham to the Said Society laid out in a picture drawn by M[r] Hogarth According to order of Council Dated the 27th day of June last

"W[m] HOGARTH

"£200."

shall conclude this chapter with the very characteristic close of the advertisement in the "Daily Advertiser" announcing their appearance, as well as the auction of the *Marriage-à-la-Mode*, of which we have already given an account. We quote from Nichols' "Genuine Works." "As (according to the standard of judgment, so righteously and laudably established by Picture-dealers, Picture-cleaners, Picture-frame-makers, and other Connoisseurs) the works of a Painter are to be esteemed more or less valuable as they are more or less scarce, and as the living Painter is most of all affected by the inferences resulting from this and other considerations equally uncandid and edifying; Mr. Hogarth, by way of precaution, not puff, begs leave to urge, that, probably, this[1] will be the last suit or series of Pictures that he may ever exhibit, because of the difficulty of vending such a number at once to any tolerable advantage, and that the whole number he has already exhibited of the historical or humourous kind does not exceed fifty, of which the three sets called 'The Harlot's Progress,' 'The Rake's Progress,' and that now to be sold, make twenty; so that whoever has a taste of his own to rely on, not too squeamish for the production of a Modern, and courage enough to own it, by daring to give them a place in his collection (till Time, the supposed finisher, but real designer of Paintings, has rendered them fit for those more sacred Repositories where Schools, Names, Heads, Masters, &c., attain their last stage of preferment), may from hence be convinced that multiplicity at least of his (Mr. Hogarth's) pieces will be no diminution of their value."

---

[1] That is, the series of *Marriage-à-la-Mode*.

CHAPTER VII.

THE "ANALYSIS," "ELECTION PRINTS," AND "SIGISMONDA."

1753 TO 1761.

IN 1753 Hogarth was fifty-six years of age. He had done his best work; and, with the exception of the *Four Prints of an Election*, produced nothing after this date worthy of the brain which contrived the *Marriage-à-la-Mode*. Horace Walpole, indeed, regards the *Credulity, Superstition, and Fanaticism* as, "for useful and deep satire," the "most sublime" of his efforts. But no doubt the note—in the followers of Wesley and Whitefield—of what Mr. Matthew Arnold calls "provinciality" was distasteful to refined Mr. Walpole; and in common with many of his contemporaries, he would probably have welcomed any capable satire on Methodism as "useful and deep." In this instance, as in others, we do not share his opinion. It is to be observed, however, that if Hogarth gave birth to no work which could add to his fame, on the other hand he issued one or two in these last years of his life which, though they now affect his reputation but little, had a great influence upon his credit at the time. Those which concern this chapter were the book called the "Analysis of Beauty," and the picture of *Sigismonda*. These two ill-starred productions gave just that opportunity to his detractors, which, so long as he confined himself to the delineation of vices and follies, was lost in the general applause. And he had many enemies. With all picture-mongery and sham-connoisseurship he was at war. His success had alienated some of his colleagues; his plain-spoken opinions some of his friends. Added to this, he was an older, perhaps a weaker man. Yet it was precisely at this period that he set himself to compose in the "Analysis" a treatise "to fix the fluctuating ideas of Taste," and sought in *Sigismonda* "to rival the ancients on their own ground." He was not a literary man in any sense (he speaks of himself as "one who never took up the pen before"); yet he selected a subject which above all requires the utmost resources of style and verbal *finesse*—the science of Æsthetics: he had won his spurs in the field of pictorial satire; yet with that strange fatality which so often betrays the wisest to their discomfiture, he hoped to compete successfully with the magic colouring of the Italians. In either case his failures were more than respectable; and they were the failures of genius; but they were failures nevertheless. Their worst result was that they embittered his remaining days; and involved him in acrimonious disputes at a time of life when he might have reasonably expected a peaceful close to his long and laborious career.

The "Analysis of Beauty" had the following origin. In the portrait of himself which Hogarth had painted in 1745,[1]—that excellent portrait in which his shrewd, sensible, blue-eyed head in its Montero cap looks out at us

---

[1] This is the date on the palette in the corner of the picture.

from the canvas in the National Gallery—he had drawn on a palette in the corner a serpentine line with these words under it, "*The Line of Beauty and Grace.*" Much inquiry, it is said, ensued as to the meaning of this hieroglyphic; and the result was that he determined to write a book to explain his symbol. That he was fully aware of the dangers of such an enterprise is humorously expressed in an epigram by himself:—

> "What!—a book, and by Hogarth!—then twenty to ten,
> All he's gain'd by the *pencil*, he'll *lose* by the pen."
> "Perhaps it may be so,—howe'er, miss or hit,
> He will publish,—*here goes—it's double or quit.*"

He also appears to have invoked the assistance of Dr. Benjamin Hoadly, Mr. Townley of Merchant Tailors' School, Mr. Ralph and others. Nevertheless, the "Analysis" did not escape some of those errors of orthography which afforded such delight to the petty criticism of the day. For the work itself, it was just such a one as might be expected under such conditions. In parts it was shrewd and sensible like the author; but wanting as a whole in method, development, precision of expression, and perhaps of idea. This makes it so difficult to describe except as a desultory essay having for pretext the not very definite precept attributed to Michael Angelo, that a figure should be always "Pyramidall, Serpent-like, and multiplied by one two and three." Its fate was exactly what might have been anticipated. The adverse critics fell with a shout upon all its obscurities and incoherencies, while the caricaturist diverted himself with representations of the ungainly "Graces" of "Painter Pugg." It is not worth while to enumerate their efforts, a number of which are fully described in Mr. F. G. Stephens' Catalogue of

"Satirical Prints and Drawings" in the British Museum. On the other hand, the friendly critics were not backward in their praises. Mr. Ralph declared that "composition is at last become a science; the student knows what he is in search of; the connoisseur what to praise; and fancy or fashion, or prescription, will usurp the hacknied name of taste no more." "Sylvanus Urban," in an ingenious copy of verses prefixed to his twenty-fourth volume (1754), refers to the "Analysis" as follows:—

> "The *Proteus* BEAUTY, that illusive pow'r,
> Who changing still, was all things in an hour,
> Now, fix'd and bound, is just what Reason wills,
> Nor wayward Fancy's wild decrees fulfills;"—

and he gave besides a long account of the work. Others, as kindly, followed suit. A translation into German was made by one Christlob Mylius in 1754, an Italian version appeared at Leghorn in 1761, and a French one at Paris in 1805 by Jansen, Talleyrand's librarian. It has not been found necessary to reprint the book of late years.

The two plates by which it was illustrated deserve a passing word. They represented a *Country Dance* and a *Statuary's Yard*, and each was set in a framework of smaller illustrations. The book itself must be consulted to make the latter perfectly intelligible; but the dance, which occupies the centre of the former, requires no lengthy explanation. It is said to represent the *Wanstead Assembly;* and to include the figures of Earl Tylney, his countess and their children, tenants, &c. In any case the dancers exhibit almost every eccentricity of posture which it is possible for the "poetry of motion" to assume. Hogarth's own comment on the plate is this:—
"The best representation in a picture, of even the most

elegant dancing, as every figure is rather a suspended action in it than an attitude, must be always somewhat unnatural and ridiculous; for were it possible in a real dance to fix every person at one instant of time, as in a picture, not one in twenty would appear to be graceful, though each were ever so much so in their movements; nor could the figure of the dance itself be at all understood." The subscription ticket to the "Analysis" was *Columbus breaking the Egg*—according to the well-known anecdote—to make it stand on end. Hogarth's object here was to call attention to the fact that, although his theory of the line of Beauty (symbolized in the design by two eels upon a plate) was old and simple, at least he was the first who had definitely announced it.

The only other prints which belong to the interval between the "Analysis" and the *Election Series* in 1755-8, are a whimsical frontispiece to Kirby's "Perspective," embodying almost every possible error in that science of which ignorance could possibly be guilty (it has been said that even ignorance would have escaped one or two of them); and the plate of *Crowns, Mitres, etc.*, already referred to in Chap. iii. This was now re-issued as a subscription ticket to the *Four Prints of an Election*, to which we now come.

The first of the series—an *Election Entertainment*—was issued in February, 1755. The general elections of the preceding year, and perhaps those at Oxford in particular, probably suggested the original paintings. This supposition is sustained by the reference in the first to the "Jew Bill" and "Marriage Act" of 1753, and to the change in the calendar of 1752 ("Give us our eleven days!"). At a couple of tables in the large room of a country inn the "yellows," or Court party, are feasting their constituents, "Speak and Have" (according to the escutcheon) being the profuse motto of the festivities. One candidate unwillingly submits to the fulsome caresses of a stout lady. The other, between the delighted fraternity of a sweep who squints, and the reeking confidences of a maudlin barber, is equally embarrassed. A stout parson, mopping his pate over a steaming chafing-dish; a long-chinned nobleman hob-a-nobbing with a long-chinned fiddler; a wag, with a face smeared on his knuckles, who sings "An Old Woman clothed in Gray" to a couple of bumpkins; an alderman in a fit from a surfeit of oysters; and an agent stunned by a brickbat from without, while he is registering the "sure" and "doubtful" votes—are some of the principal guests.

In another part of the plate an incorruptible Methodist tailor is plied at once by agent, wife, and son. In the foreground a butcher with "*pro patria*" bound on his broken head pours Geneva on the green wound of a wincing bludgeon-man, who takes a dram of the same remedy internally; a frightened boy brews rack punch in a tub; and a squat pedlar distrustfully eyes a promissory note received in payment for his wares. Finally, a sword is seen leaving the room at the head of a posse of cudgels. These are only a few of the incidents in this "matchless picture," as Charles Lamb calls it.

The second scene shows the *Canvassing for Votes*. Upon a show-cloth, which hangs before the "Royal Oak," a stream of secret service money pours from the Treasury (with which the artist has maliciously contrasted Ware's stunted Horse Guards); and Punch, ministerial "candidate for Guzzledown," scatters the golden shower among eager electors. Yet, notwithstanding this home-thrust at the

FRONTISPIECE TO "KIRBY'S PERSPECTIVE."

corrupt practices of the "yellows," the "blue" landlord may be seen below contending with his rival of the "Crown" for the vote of a newly arrived farmer, who is slyly taking the bribes of both. Behind, an electioneering agent (Mr. Tim Partytool), by judicious gifts from a Jew-pedlar's tray, is securing the good offices of some girls in the balcony. Those of the landlady, whose counted gains are watched by a covetous grenadier, have been already insured. The same may be inferred of a dumpy cobbler on the left of the picture, who, with a finger on his newly acquired guineas, listens unconvinced to the noisy narrative which a barber, aided by sundry bits of tobacco pipe, is giving of Vernon's popular capture of Porto Bello (figured by a quart-pot), "with six ships only." In the background, before the "Crown" (also the Excise Office), a riotous crowd are tugging at the sign, which a man is sawing through in blissful ignorance that its fall involves his own destruction. An old figure-head of a Lion swallowing a Fleur-de-lis, which stands in front of the "Royal Oak," alludes to the war with France which broke out in 1755, and was greatly fomented by the country party.

The *Polling* follows the *Canvassing*, and the set finishes with the *Chairing of the Members*. In the *Polling*, matters are nearing their termination, as the reserve voters are being brought up to the hustings, and the worn-out constable is dozing. Fortune, whether "blue" or "yellow," is clearly in favour of one of the candidates, whose complacent attitude is being caricatured. The other scratches his head in manifest discomfiture, while a ballad-woman in front retails an uncomplimentary broadside, which no doubt refers to him.

A battered pensioner, who has lost an arm, a leg and a

G

hand in Queen Anne's wars, is the first at the polling-place. He lays his iron hook on the Bible. The lawyers wrangle as to the validity of the oath; the clerk explodes with merriment. Next the soldier, an idiot with a bib, confined in his chair by a wooden bar, votes at the prompting of a man in fetters, the infamous Dr. Shebbeare, who was imprisoned and pilloried for libelling George I., and whose sixth "Letter to the people of England" peeps from his pocket. Behind, a half-dead hospital patient with "true blue" in his cap is borne up the steps between a nurse and a noseless wretch, the fumes of whose pipe curl in the face of his ghastly burden. A blind man follows, carelessly guided by a gaping boy, and a cripple brings up the rear. In the background, under a bridge occupied by an uproarious electioneering procession, Britannia's coach breaks down while the unheeding coachman and footman play cards upon the box.

Chairing the Members, the last of the series, would appear at first sight to be a misnomer, as one only is shown. But the shadow of the other appears upon a wall at the back. The gentleman whose triumph occupies the picture clearly belongs to the "blue" or country party (see "True Blue" on the banner). Hogarth afterwards held a Court appointment; but, although he has distributed his satire pretty equally, his sympathies in this case were probably with the "blues."

The procession is in disorder. A frightened sow, preceded by her litter, one of which is drowning, has broken the ranks. The backstroke of a flail wielded by a thresher in front strikes one of the chair-bearers, who, tottering, increases the confusion. The unhappy member, said to be the borough-monger Bubb Dodington, clings desperately

to the arms of his wavering chair; a lady, who watches him from the church, faints with terror, and the "yellows" in the window (among whom is the old Duke of Newcastle) enjoy his misery. In imitation of the eagle above Alexander in Le Brun's *Battle of the* **Granicus** a goose flies over his head.

The thresher who causes so much mischief is engaged in a conflict with a sailor leading a bear. The bear seizes the opportunity of plundering the barrels of an ass, whose master retaliates with a cudgel, while the terrified wriggling of a monkey on Bruin's back discharges a toy-gun in the face of a grinning sweep, who is fixing gingerbread spectacles on a stone skull.

We have still left much undescribed in this capital series, but the original pictures are luckily still in existence. They are among the best examples of Hogarth's style, broadly and freshly painted. Garrick purchased them for 200 guineas. From him they passed in 1823 to Sir John Soane, in whose museum at Lincoln's Inn Fields they are at present. The price then paid for them was £1,732 10s.

In 1756 Hogarth made a final essay in historical painting, and so far as money is concerned, the effort was wholly successful. For the Altarpiece of St. Mary Redcliffe at Bristol he received £500. The compartments represented the *Sealing of the Sepulchre*, the *Ascension* and the *Three Maries*; and are now in the Fine Arts Academy at Clifton.

One or two minor prints require to be noticed before we come to the *Sigismonda*. In the above-mentioned year, when people were much exercised by fears of the threatened invasion of England by France,—when a camp was formed in Surrey, and a " Great Personage " at Kensington (according to the " Gentleman's Magazine ") went so far as to say that 10,000 French were actually embarking, Hogarth—doubtless still sorely conscious of his Calais mishap—contributed his version of the " present posture of affairs " in a couple of prints entitled *The Invasion, or France and England.* The subjects might almost be guessed. The French are shown as half-starved frog-eaters, forced unwillingly to embark from their depopulated country—the only really cheerful person in the picture being a sanguinary monk, who presides over the shipment of various engines of Popish torture to be employed at a proposed monastery "*dans Black Friars a Londre.*" The English, on the other hand, are jubilant at the prospect of their adversaries' arrival. Hodge (for whose portrait it is reported that Garrick stood) strains along the sergeant's halberd to reach the regulation height, whilst a brawny grenadier is decorating the wall of the "Duke of Cumberland" with a fine fresco of Louis the Well-Beloved, from whose lips, in allusion to the gasconading memorial of M. Rouille to Fox, issues a label:—" You take a my fine ships, you be de Pirate, you be de Teef, me send my grand Armies, & hang you all, Morblu." In earnest of which he flourishes a gibbet. Garrick wrote some verses for these prints ; but they have no special merit, though they are better than Dr. John Hoadly's to the *Harlot's Progress.*

The print called *The Bench* (Sept. 4, 1758) requires no lengthy notice. It is said to contain the portraits of the Honourable William Noel, Sir Edward Clive, Sir John Willes, Lord Chief Justice, and the Honourable Mr. (afterwards Earl) Bathurst, and was designed to show the difference between " Character," " Caricature," and "Outré."

"Character" only is represented in the first state of print. In the second state is added at the top a row of heads expressing "Caricature" and "Outré;" but **they were** never finished. Another print, dated November 5, 1759, shows the old *Cockpit* in Bird Cage Walk (?) with **all the "celestial** anarchy and confusion" which, according **to Sherlock,** characterized the pastime **of which it was** the theatre. Jockeys and cockbreeders, **sweeps** and Quakers, English Dukes and French Marquises, **blind** men and deaf **men,** are absorbed **in this** exciting **sport.** A defaulter, whose shadow alone **is seen, has,** according to Cockpit law, been drawn **up to the** ceiling in a basket, whence he vainly tenders **his watch to satisfy** his creditors. **This** is one of the best **of Hogarth's later prints; but we** cannot dwell upon it.

On the 6th of June, 1757, Hogarth **was** appointed Serjeant Painter of all his Majesty's Works "as well belonging to his Royal Palaces or houses **as** to his great Wardrobe **or** otherwise." He succeeded his brother-in-law, the **John** Thornhill of the "Five Days' **Tour;"** and from **an** autograph note in **the** Forster collection, **entered upon his** duties **on the** 16th of July. The salary **by the warrant** was £10 per annum, payable quarterly; but there **were** apparently **certain "fees,** liveries, profits, commodities **and** advantages" **which** made it rather more. In one **of the** memoranda **printed** by Ireland, he says that it "might not have exceeded one hundred a year to me for trouble and attendance; but, by two portraits, at more than eighty pounds each, the last occasioned by his present Majesty's accession, and some other things, it has, for these last five years been, one **way** or other, worth two hundred pounds *per ann.*"

Although in 1757 he had, **in** a fit of irritation, announced that he should in future "employ the rest of his time in portrait painting," he appears about 1759-60 to have rather inconsistently "determined to quit the pencil for the graver." "In this humble walk (he says) I had one advantage; the perpetual fluctuations in the manners of the times enabled me to introduce new characters, which being drawn from the passing day, had a chance of more originality and less insipidity than those which are repeated again and again, and again, from old stories. Added to this, the prints which I had previously engraved were now become a voluminous work, and circulated not only through England, but over Europe. These being secured to me by an Act which I had previously got passed, were a kind of an estate; and as they wore, I could repair and re-touch them; so that in some particulars they became better than when first engraved.

'While I was making arrangements to confine myself entirely to my graver, an amiable nobleman (Lord Charlemont) requested that before I bade a final adieu to the pencil, I would paint him one picture. The subject [was] to be my own choice, and the reward,—whatever I demanded. The story I pitched upon was a young and virtuous married lady, who, by playing at cards with an officer, loses her money, watch and jewels; the moment when he offers them back in return for her honour, and she is wavering at his suit, was my point of time."

The picture thus indicated is that known as the *Lady's Last Stake*, or *Picquet*, or *Virtue in Danger*. It was engraved by Cheeseman in 1825; and a copy of the print was given for the first time in Bell and Daldy's two-volume Hogarth of 1872. Lord Charlemont, for whom it was painted, was greatly delighted with it; and John

Ireland has printed a couple of letters on the subject which show this nobleman in a very favourable light. To Hogarth's description of the design it is only necessary to add that the heroine is a portrait of Mrs. Piozzi, then Miss Salusbury.[1]

During the process of painting, the *Lady's Last Stake* had found other admirers; and by one of them, Sir Richard (afterwards Lord) Grosvenor, Hogarth was pressed to undertake another picture "upon the same terms." He selected Dryden's (or rather Boccaccio's) *Sigismonda* weeping over the heart of her murdered lover Guiscardo, —the choice of subject being apparently determined by the large price given for a picture having the same theme, ascribed to Correggio, but really by Furini, which had been sold for £400 with Sir Luke Schaub's collection in 1758.[2] Hogarth valued his picture at the same sum, and took immense pains with it, touching and retouching it in obedience to the suggestions of his friends. When it was finished, Sir Richard had either, as the painter surmises, got into the hands of the picture-dealers, or repented of his commission. At all events he appears to have rather meanly shuffled out of it, upon the plea that "the constantly having it [the picture] before one's eyes would be too often occasioning melancholy ideas to arise in one's mind."[3] *Sigismonda*, therefore, greatly to the artist's

---

[1] This picture was sold at Christie's, in 1874, for £1,585. Lord Charlemont gave the painter £100.

[2] It was exhibited at Manchester in 1857 (No. 348). It is now— according to Cunningham's "Letters of Horace Walpole"—in the possession of the Duke of Newcastle, at Clumber.

[3] Hogarth has humorously paraphrased Sir Richard's excuse in some verses addressed to Dr. Hay, and "turned," says he, "into English by

mortification, was left upon his hands. This unfortunate transaction of course gave rise to much contemporary criticism, sadly envenomed by party-feeling and professional antagonism. One result was that not being sold to Sir Richard Grosvenor, it was not sold to any one else. After Hogarth's death, it remained in the possession of his widow, with an injunction that she was not to part with it for less than £500 during her lifetime; but when she died in 1789 it passed into the possession of Messrs. Boydell, who bought it for 56 guineas. At that time it had not been engraved, although Hogarth had made several fruitless attempts to secure an adequate interpreter, and had even issued as a subscription ticket the admirable little plate of *Time smoking a Picture*, 1761. In 1793 it was reproduced in mezzotint by Dunkarton, and subsequently, in 1795, by Bartolozzi's pupil, Benjamin Smith.

At this date there is no doubt that the picture was not fairly treated in the painter's life-time. The mob of dealers heaped it with obloquy, and the caricaturists rejoiced in a new opportunity of reviling the unpopular author of the *Analysis*. Then Mr. Walpole, summing up in his "Anecdotes of Painting," declared that it was "no more like Sigismonda than he to Hercules," and it may perhaps be

---

my friend Whitehead"—the Paul Whitehead of Churchill's satires. Here are the lines in question :—

> "Nay; 'tis so moving, that the knight
> Cant bear the figure in his sight;—
> And who would tears so dearly buy
> As give four hundred pounds to cry?
> I own, he chose the prudent part,
> Rather to break his word than heart;
> And yet, methinks, 'tis ticklish dealing,
> With one so delicate—in feeling."

conceded that there was not the slightest resemblance between Mr. Walpole and Alcmena's son. Worse than this, he wrote of it in terms which were, if not absolutely untrue, at least exaggerated and unjustifiable; and the "common cry" of critics followed the example of the illustrious *virtuoso* of Strawberry Hill. But those who care to form an opinion of their own, and who, to use Hogarth's own recommendation,

> " To Nature and Themselves appeal,
> Nor learn of others what to feel."

can decide for themselves on visiting the National Gallery, where, by bequest of the late Mr. Anderdon, this much abused picture has found a permanent resting-place. They may not be inclined to rank it with Correggio, as its designer intended, but they will probably admit that it is soundly painted, full of technical skill and in excellent preservation. Considering that the attempt was made in a direction so unfavourable to the peculiar cast of the artist's talent, it is wonderful that he succeeded so well. Nevertheless, since the enterprise was undertaken with so little profit to his peace or reputation, it cannot but be regretted that he ever made the attempt.

Both *Sigismonda* and the *Lady's Last Stake*, with the *Election Entertainment* and some other of Hogarth's pictures, were exhibited at Spring Gardens in 1761. For the catalogue of this exhibition, the story of which is too lengthy to tell in this place, and which may, moreover, be read in most histories of the Royal Academy, Hogarth executed a "head" and "tail-piece," which were engraved by Grignion. The former represents Britannia watering the three young trees of "Painting," "Sculpture," and "Architecture," from a fountain surmounted by a bust of George III., "emblematical of the confident hope entertained that native talent in art would be cherished by royal patronage." "*Et spes et ratio studiorum in Cæsare tantum*" was its motto. The **tail-piece**, directed at **wealthy collectors**, is an admirable figure of a travelled monkey **with an** eye-glass, watering the stumps of three dead trees **in pots labelled** "Exotics." Hogarth had evidently not **forgotten that the** *virtuosi* **had** allowed the *Marriage-à-la-Mode* **to be sold for (as Sir Martin** Shee phrases it in his "Rhymes on Art") **"a sum too** contemptible to be named." These plates made the **catalogue,** which also contained an allegorical design by **Wale, very popular,** and not less than thirteen thousand **copies were sold.** The price was a shilling.

CHAPTER THE LAST.

WILKES AND CHURCHILL. DEATH. CONCLUSION.

1762 TO 1764.

IN March, 1762, Hogarth issued the plate known as *Credulity, Superstition, and Fanaticism. A Medley.* It was an extension, or perhaps we should say adaptation, of a previous design entitled *Enthusiasm Delineated*, of which only two impressions exist.[1] *Credulity, Superstition, and Fanaticism* is, in fact, simply *Enthusiasm Delineated* re-engraved upon the same copper; but the alterations were so numerous as practically to make the former an entirely new design. As this is the one which Hogarth chose to give to the world, it is with this alone that we have to do; but it is always serviceable to trace the progress of invention in an artist's mind; and, therefore, following the majority of our predecessors, we shall begin by describing *Enthusiasm Delineated*. The artist intended—he says— to give in this plate "a lineal representation of the strange effects of literal and low conceptions of sacred beings, as also of the idolatrous tendency of pictures in churches

---

[1] One of these is in the British Museum; the other, long in the possession of the late Mr. White of Brownlow Street, was recently sold at Christie's. John Ireland published a copy by Isaac Mills in 1795.

and prints in religious books." Accordingly, from a pulpit decorated with dangling puppets of Moses and Aaron, Peter, Paul, and Adam and Eve, an energetic elocutionist (who, by the scale of vociferation at his side, has reached "Bull roar") is declaiming to a motley congregation, whose extraordinary vagaries are watched through the window by an astounded Mahometan. Under the preacher's gown is a harlequin suit; under his wig, which flies off in his gesticulation (carrying away its attendant " glory " with it) is the tonsure of a Jesuit. In one hand, to give force to his denunciations, he holds forth a bearded figure with the symbol of the Trinity; in the other is a devil with a gridiron. In the pew below a minute ghostly personage is collecting the tears of a repentant thief in a bottle. The other occupants of the pew, a nobleman and a girl, have apparently thrown aside their celestial exemplar for a more earthly teacher. A dog under the reading-desk, with "G. Whitfield" on his collar, howls melodiously to the psalmody of a cherub-flanked clerk above, in whom some have recognized Whitefield himself. A convulsed woman in the corner is said to be intended for Mother Douglas of the Piazza (Foote's "Mother Cole"), who ended her life in those pious exercises which Fate and the pillory denied to Mother Needham of the *Harlot's Progress*. Behind, a sweep is embracing an image, while a Jew, in a moment of exaltation, sacrifices an obtrusive insect. In the background a number of figures, in ridicule of the doctrine of Transubstantiation, are eating the little images which they hold. We omit other details, which must be studied in the engraving.

This was Hogarth's first thought, and his language was forcible enough. In the second design, *Credulity, Superstition, and Fanaticism*, most of its chief features are altered to suit the modified purpose indicated in the title, and scarcely ever strengthened or improved. For the symbolical figure of the Trinity is substituted a witch on a broomstick, while Cæsar, Sir George Villiers and Defoe's "Mrs. Veal" take the place of the scriptural puppets round the pulpit. The fervent couple in the pew beneath are metamorphosed into two ordinary personages, and in lieu of the penitent thief we have a pair of figures, to one of whom a diminutive devil is whispering. As instances of credulity the Bilston nail-spouter and the Godalming rabbit-breeder (Mary Tofts, a notorious impostor in 1726-7) are put instead of Mother Douglas and the sweep, while King James's " Demonology " and Whitefield's " Journal " appear on the hassock formerly occupied by the dog. There are other alterations which it is impossible to enumerate. Probably the painter's advisers, fearing lest his intentions should be misconstrued, recommended him to expunge some of the apparent irreverences of his first design, and this may have given rise to the modification of the whole idea, a modification so substantial as to change what was a compact satire into a desultory work which the artist properly styled "a Medley"—a work of genius for a lesser man, but scarcely worthy of Hogarth, for all that Walpole regards it as the "most sublime of his works for useful and deep satire." The praise would have been more fitly applied to *Enthusiasm Delineated*, which the critic does not appear to have seen.

We come now to the last notable event in Hogarth's life—the publication of *The Times* and the quarrel with Wilkes and Churchill. Long before the death of George II. Hogarth is supposed to have enjoyed the favour of Lord Bute. Up to this date, however, he had avoided politics; but shortly before Bute's accession to the Premiership in 1762 the general stagnation and an evil genius prompted him to project some "timed" thing in the ministerial interest. The announcement of his purpose at once brought him into collision with the demagogue John Wilkes, then editor of the opposition "North Briton," and Churchill the poet, with both of whom he had lived on terms of some intimacy. Wilkes endeavoured to prevent the appearance of the print by threatening reprisals; Hogarth refused to desist and—in John Ireland's words—the black flag was hoisted on both sides. Under these circumstances *The Times* (Pl. i.) was published, Sept. 7, 1762.

This "World" public-house is on fire. Pitt on stilts, as the tyrant Henry VIII., and having, in allusion to his pension, a millstone inscribed with £3,000 hanging from his neck, is exciting the flames; while Bute, played upon by a featureless man (Lord Temple), and a brace of garreteers (Wilkes and Churchill), is directing the hose of an engine worked by Highlanders, soldiers, and sailors. A Grub-street hack with a barrowful of "Monitors" and "North Britons" endeavours to cut the supply pipe. The sign of the "Newcastle Inn" is falling down (the Duke had resigned in May), and an incendiary with a knife in his pocket is hoisting in its stead the "Patriot Arms"—four fists clenched and opposed. To the right Frederick of Prussia fiddles among his weeping subjects, while to the left a Dutchman, behind whom a fox peeps out of a kennel, sits on a bale watching the proceedings. There are other allusions, many of them pointed, to contemporary events; but the whole composition is somewhat laboured, and the central idea is scarcely novel.

Wilkes kept his word as to reprisals. On the Saturday following the issue of the above satire, the seventeenth number of the "North Briton" appeared, headed by a rough woodcut portrait of Hogarth, and containing a violent attack upon his character, both as a man and an artist. The alleged decay of his powers—the miscarriage of the *Sigismonda*—the cobbled composition of the *Analysis*—were all discussed with scurrilous malignity by one who had known his domestic life and learned his weaknesses. There can be little doubt that Hogarth was deeply wounded. "Being," he says, "at that time very weak, and in a kind of slow fever, it could not but seize on a feeling mind." His assailant believed that he had killed him, and wrote to Lord Temple that he was dying.

The painter, however, was far from dead, although he appears to have deferred his retaliation till he could make it more directly personal. When, in the May of the following year, Wilkes was brought to Westminster Hall upon his trial for libel, Hogarth sketched his portrait. Nature had not favoured the patriotic colonel of the Buckinghamshire militia, and it has been gravely argued that this squinting semblance of him, like the sketch of Lord Lovat, was only intended as a portrait. But the reference in it to the attack upon himself, and the subscription to the subsequent plate of Churchill, clearly show that Hogarth intended to exhibit the worthless character of the man through his features. If this really resembled Wilkes, and Wilkes himself allowed it did, he must have carried in his face a confirmation of the worst vices that have been laid to his charge.

It would have been well for Hogarth if the matter could have ended here. But Churchill, who, as appears from a letter to Garrick printed by Mr. Forster,[1] had been planning an "Epistle to William Hogarth" ever since the appearance of *The Times*, now published his attack upon the painter. It was a slashing and savage performance, unequal like most of Churchill's work, and seeing that it fell hardest upon Hogarth's age and failing powers, scarcely worthy of his generally manly muse. It contains, however, a well-known tribute to the artist's genius which has out-lived its hostile invective:—

> "In walks of Humour, in that cast of Style,
> Which, probing to the quick, yet makes us smile;
> In Comedy, his nat'ral road to fame,
> Nor let me call it by a meaner name,
> Where a beginning, middle, and an end
> Are aptly joined; where parts on parts depend,
> Each made for each, as bodies for their soul,
> So as to form one true and perfect whole,
> Where a plain Story to the eye is told,
> Which we conceive the moment we behold,
> Hogarth unrivall'd stands, and shall engage
> Unrivall'd praise to the most distant age."

To Churchill's "Epistle" of July, Hogarth rejoined, on the 1st of August following, by a print entitled *The Bruiser, C. Churchill (once the Reverend!) in the character of a Russian Hercules regaling himself after having killed the monster Caricatura, that so severely galled his virtuous friend, the heaven-born Wilkes.*" The poet appears as a bear, with torn bands and ruffles, hugging a club, the knots of which are inscribed "Lye 1, Lye 2, etc.," and "regaling himself" with a quart pot of his favourite beverage, "British Burgundy." The portrait is propped on Massinger's "New Way to Pay Old Debts," and "A list of the Subscribers to the 'North

---

[1] See also Garrick's letter to Churchill, quoted at p. 63.

Briton.'" To intimate the poverty of those who wrote this last, the pile is crowned by a padlocked begging box.

To a later issue of this the painter added a tablet, in which he is represented with a whip, teaching Wilkes and Churchill to dance while Temple fiddles. Pitt, flanked by Gog and Magog (his City supporters), and having the millstone of *The Times* (Pl. i.) suspended above his head by a thread, fires a mortar at the dove of peace, but the ball drops short. "The pleasure, and pecuniary advantage," says Hogarth, "which I derived from these two engravings [of Wilkes and Churchill], together with occasionally riding on horseback, restored me to as much health as can be expected at my time of life."

"Thus" (and here conclude the autobiographical notes from which we have so often quoted) "have I gone through the principal circumstances of a life which, till lately, past pretty much to my own satisfaction, and, I hope, in no respect injurious to any other man. This I can safely assert, I have invariably endeavoured to make those about me tolerably happy, and my greatest enemy cannot say I ever did an intentional injury; though, without ostentation, I could produce many instances of men that have been essentially benefited by me. What may follow, God knows.
Finis."

There is not much more to tell of Hogarth's life. A plate entitled *The Times* (Pl. ii.) was prepared in 1762; but its publication then was abandoned for unknown reasons. It appeared after Mrs. Hogarth's death, when the Boydells published it. But by that time the allusions had grown

---

[1] The original pen-and-ink sketch of Wilkes, and a little memorandum-book containing, among other things, a rough pencil sketch for the *Bruiser* are now in the possession of Mr. Frederick Locker.

obscure; and there would be no good end served now in describing a design which enters into the list of Hogarth's works merely as a curiosity. In the same year he produced a portrait of his friend Dr. Morell and that pen-and-ink sketch from memory which, with the exception of a miniature copied in Nichols's "Literary Anecdotes of the Eighteenth Century," is all that we possess in the way of a semblance of Henry Fielding. These, with the frontispiece to Clubbe's "Physiognomy," entitled the *Weighing House*, bring us to the print of *Finis*, or *The Bathos*.

A few months before he died Hogarth set to work to prepare a "tailpiece" to his works, then numerous enough to form a bulky volume. With a presentiment that his life was nearing its close he informed his friends that he had chosen for his subject the *End of all things*, and true to his creed, his last work (to which, in imitation of Swift's "Art of Sinking in Poetry," he gave the title of *The Bathos, or Manner of Sinking in Sublime Painting*) is a blow at his ancient enemies, the old masters, whose occasional pettinesses and incongruities he ridicules in this jumbled assemblage of fag-ends. Supported by the fragment of a column, Time, *moriturus*, with shattered scythe and glass, exhales the final puff from his pipe, which breaks as it falls from his nerveless hand. By the will at his side he has devised his worldly goods to Chaos his "sole Executor," and the Fates are witness. Nature is bankrupt; Apollo lies dead in his chariot; the sign of the "World's End" is falling, the ship sinks, the trees are withered, and the moon is dark. A play-book open at *Exeunt omnes*; an empty money-bag; "a shoemaker's last and a cobbler's end;" the remnants of a crown; a halter and a stringless bow; a cracked bell and a broken bottle; a broom stump

and a gunstock without a barrel, litter the foreground. *The Times* (Pl. i.), the cause of so much heart-burning, crackles and parches in the flame of a candle-end, and the palette of the painter has done its work.

Under this print to left and right are two **figures in circles.** One represents the "**conic** Form" under **which Venus** was worshipped at **Paphos; the** other the cone and "line of Beauty" from the *Analysis* (Pl. i. fig. 26). The identity of these two figures, we learn from an inscription on the print, "did **not** occur to the Author till two or three years **after the** publication of the *Analysis* in 1754 [3]." It **must have** been about this time that he made use of the former for the crest,[1] of which we possess the sketch designed by him for Catton the coach-painter; and, if we may infer that he then first set up his carriage, **it is** clear that he could not have done so much before **1756** or 1757.

The Bathos was Hogarth's **last** published work. Indeed if **we** except some additions made to *The Bench*, he never **touched** pencil more. It was published in March, 1764. On **the 25th** of October in the same year he was conveyed from **his house at** Chiswick to Leicester Fields, very weak, but **remarkably cheerful,** and (says Nichols), "receiving an agreeable **letter from** the *American* Dr. *Franklin*, drew up a rough draft of an answer to it; but going to bed, **he was**

---

[1] The crest in question was engraved by Livesay in 1782. It consists of a scroll-work design enclosing the word *Cyprus*, and surmounted by the Cyprian cone. Beneath, on a ribbon, is the word *Variety*. A lengthy account of it will be found in "Notes and Queries" for Feb. 22, 1879. It is from the pen of the author of a recent volume on "Cruikshank." Mr. William Bates of Birmingham, who has of late years contributed many interesting "Hogarthiana" to the pages of "N. and Q."

seized with a vomiting, upon which he rung his bell with such violence that he broke it, and expired about two hours afterwards in the arms of Mrs. *Mary Lewis*, who was called up on his being taken suddenly ill." He was buried in Chiswick Churchyard, where a monument was erected to him by his friends in 1771, on one side of which, under a design representing a mask, laurel wreath, maulstick, palette, pencils, and a book inscribed "Analysis of Beauty," is an epitaph by Garrick, of which the following is an accurate copy :—

"Farewel, great Painter of Mankind!
   Who reach'd the noblest point of Art,
Whose *pictur'd Morals* charm the Mind,
   And through the Eye correct the Heart.

"If *Genius* fire thee, Reader, stay:
   If *Nature* touch thee, drop a Tear;
If neither move thee, turn away,
   For HOGARTH's honour'd dust lies here."

From a passage in Mrs. Piozzi it has been supposed that the well-known but generally misquoted quatrain by Johnson :—

"The Hand of Art here torpid lies
   That traced the essential form of Grace;
Here Death has closed the curious eyes
   That saw the manners in the face;"

was also an attempt at an epitaph by the "great Cham of Literature" which was rejected in favour of Garrick's. But it is clear from a letter in Croker's Boswell that Johnson's lines were only a suggested emendation of Garrick's verses, which had been submitted to him for criticism.

By Hogarth's will, which was dated the 16th August, 1764, he left all his property to his wife. It seems to

HOGARTH'S TOMB AT CHISWICK.

have consisted principally of his "engraved copper-plates;" and it was moreover chargeable with an annuity of £80 to his surviving sister Anne, who died in 1771, and besides minor legacies, **with one of** £100 **to** the afore-mentioned Mary Lewis. His estate must, however, **have** included the house at Chiswick,[1] for we find Mrs. Hogarth subsequently bequeathing "all that my copyhold estate, lying and being at Chiswick in Middlesex" to her "cousin Mary Lewis." She appears to have continued to rent the "Golden Head" after her husband's death, since in Nichols's editions of 1781, 1782, and 1785 he speaks of the same Mary Lewis as continuing to dispose of the prints "at Mrs. Hogarth's house in Leicester Square." Mrs. Hogarth certainly let lodgings there, for Livesay the engraver was one of her tenants in 1781-82; and Mr. Dutton Cook in a pleasant paper in "Once a Week" for December 20, 1860, gives an account of another inmate *circa* 1772, the Scotch painter **Alexander Runciman.** It is probable, however, that in her **last years** Mrs. Hogarth resided principally at Chiswick, where **Sir** Richard Phillips saw her in his boyhood, and long after drew a vivid picture of the stately old lady sailing up the aisle of the parish church, with her silk sacque, raised head-dress, black calash and crooked cane, accompanied by a relative, and preceded by her grey-haired man-servant Samuel, who, after wheeling his mistress to church in her Bath-chair,

---

[1] When Hogarth first took this house at Chiswick is not clear. Dr. Morell says, in a letter printed by the elder Nichols—"I knew little of Hogarth before he came to Chiswick, *not long after his marriage*" [1729]; and this coincides with the statement, in the "Memoir" of Cary, that it was previously the residence of Sir James Thornhill, who died in 1734. Clerk says he *purchased* it about 1743; Nichols soon after 1748, and that he passed the greater part of the summer season there.

carried in the prayer-books and shut the pew-door. In those days, though her dignity remained, her means must have considerably fallen off. Notwithstanding that by a special Act of Parliament the **copyright in her** husband's prints had been secured to **her personally for twenty** years, their sale had gradually declined; **and she was glad to** accept a pension of £40 at the **hands of the Royal** Academy, who granted it upon the interposition **of the** king. When she **died** in 1789, she left all she had **to** Mary Lewis, **who shortly** afterwards, in consideration of a life annuity, **transferred** her right in the copper-plates to Messrs. **Boydell.** The Chiswick house reverted at Mary Lewis's death in 1808 to other persons named by Mrs. Hogarth. **From 1814** to 1826 it was inhabited by the Rev. H. F. Cary, the translator of Dante, who during that period held the curacy and lectureship of Chiswick. Another resident was Mr. N. T. Hicks, the well-known melodramatic actor. When the writer last saw it, not many months ago, it was occupied by a very humble tenantry, and sadly dilapidated. The old mulberry tree, **once** braced and girdled by Hogarth's fostering care, still **drags on** an amputated existence, and produces fruit in good **seasons;** but the tombs of Pompey the dog, and Dick the **Bullfinch,** the latter rudely graved by the painter himself with **the** end of a nail, have disappeared, while the roomy garden, **which in** Mary Lewis's time was "laid out in a good style," **is** now neglected. Nevertheless the place is well worth a pilgrimage for Hogarth's sake; and **those** Londoners who care for an afternoon to shake—

"to all the liberal air
The dust and din and steam of town"

may do worse than **spend** it in visiting the tumbledown red-brick villa with the bay window on the road to Chiswick gardens, and the old tomb in Chiswick Churchyard piously repaired in 1856 by "William Hogarth of Aberdeen."[1]

There are several portraits of Hogarth, most of them from his own hand. The best is that in the National Gallery (No. 112), in which he is shown as a blue-eyed, intelligent little man, in a Montero cap. (Leigh Hunt says he has "a sort of knowing jockey look," and the phrase is not wholly inapt.) The canvas rests upon three volumes labelled respectively "Shakespeare," "Milton," and "Swift," and his favourite pug-dog Trump sits at the right of it. In the left corner is a palette inscribed "The Line of Beauty and Grace, W. H. 1745,"—the famous inscription which gave rise to the *Analysis*; and it was the "old plate" of this portrait with a "background and a dog ready" which Hogarth made use of in 1763 for his print of "Master Churchill in the character of a Bear." Another portrait is that of *Hogarth painting the Comic Muse*, now in the National Portrait Gallery, in which he sits before his easel in profile. It was engraved in 1758. Others are the head in a hat from the "Gate of Calais;" the oval head begun by Wheltdon, and finished by Hogarth himself; the head in a tiewig prefixed to vol. i. of Samuel Ireland's "Graphic Illustrations," a copy of which forms our frontispiece; the woodcut with a pipe in Major's Wal-

---

[1] Sketches of the house and tomb appeared in the "Pictorial World" for Sept. 26, 1874. That of the latter is here given. There were also some illustrations in the "Graphic" for Nov. 14 in the same year. In addition to these, an interesting drawing by Mr. Charles J. Staniland, showing the garden before it was subjected to modern "improvement," was published in the "Illustrated London News" for Oct. 18, 1873.

pole's "Anecdotes," and the drawing by Worlidge, which appears as a frontispiece to "Clavis Hogarthiana." Roubilliac the sculptor also executed a bust of him,[1] which is engraved in vol. ii. of Nichols's "Hogarth," 1799, and he modelled Trump the dog. To conclude the list it may be added that Hogarth painted an excellent likeness of his wife, which was exhibited at the "Old Masters" in 1873, portraits of Sir James and Lady Thornhill and their son John, his own sisters Mary and Anne, Mrs. Mary Lewis and his five servants.

There is no need in this place to attempt any elaborate verbal portrait of William Hogarth. Numerous anecdotes respecting him have been retained; but most of them come to us, if not from a tainted source, at least through a tainted channel.[2] It has been thought essential to catalogue his errors in spelling; and to collect examples of coarseness from his various productions. We shall not scruple to neglect this branch of the subject. But, in truth, there is no special difficulty about his character. Any one who had been in his company an hour was probably as well informed of his peculiarities as his oldest friends. He was—it was easy to see—a sturdy, outspoken, honest, obstinate, pugnacious little man, who, as we are glad to think, once pummelled a fellow soundly for maltreating the handsome Drummeress of *Southwark Fair*. He was

---

[1] This is in the National Portrait Gallery at South Kensington.

[2] We refer to George Steevens. It is only necessary to read this writer's abominable attack on poor Mary Lewis, whose only error appears to have been fidelity to Hogarth's memory, to judge of the value of records transmitted through such a medium. See Nichols's "Anecdotes" *passim*,—and for the special passage above referred to, pp. 113-14 of the ed. of 1785.

witty and genial as a companion; and to those he cared for thoroughly faithful and generous. He liked good clothes, good living, good order in his household; and he was proud of the rewards of industry and respectability. As a master he was exacting in his demands, but punctual in his payments; as a servant he did a good day's work, and insisted upon his hire. His prejudices, like those of most self-educated men, were strong; and he fought doggedly in defence of them without any attempt to conciliate his opponent or convince himself. That he **was not proof** against flattery seems to have been true: it is equally true of Garrick and Richardson, and a hundred others who console themselves for their enemies by their parasites. In his own walk he had succeeded by a course of training which would have failed with nineteen men out of twenty; **and he** consequently undervalued the **teaching of all academies** whatsoever. It is obvious **that with the art-patronage** and connoisseurship of his day he was **hopelessly** at war; he saw in it only the fostering of exotic models at the expense of native talent. But **a great deal** that has been said on the subject of his **attitude** to foreign schools of painting has been manifestly exaggerated; and, under any circumstances, much must be allowed for the excitement of controversy. An artist of Hogarth's parts could not be wholly insensible to the Great Masters, as some have supposed. Yet it may well be conceived **that such** a downright and quick-tongued disputant, **in** his impatience at the parrot raptures of ordinary persons, might **easily** come to utter " blasphemous expressions against the divinity even of Raphael Urbino, Correggio, and Michael Angelo." His true attitude towards them is we think disclosed in his words to Mrs. Piozzi. He was talking to her, late in life, of Dr. Johnson, whose conversation, he said, was to that of other men like Titian's painting compared to Hudson's,—"but don't you tell people now, that I say so (continued he), for the connoisseurs and I are at war you know; and because I hate *them*, they think I hate *Titian*—and let them!"

To this contest with the connoisseurs, coupled perhaps with the slender facilities for exhibiting works of art, is no doubt to be attributed that mistaken contemporary notion as to his merits as a painter. So completely had this gained ground, that even his friend Dr. Morell, writing of *Sigismonda*, says, "it is granted that colouring was not *Mr. Hogarth's* forte." But Time has modified that unjust sentence. It is now, on the contrary, granted that he *had* great merit as a painter, that his colouring is pure and harmonious, his handling singularly direct and dexterous, and that for ease and perspicuity his composition leaves nothing to be desired.

A very necessary distinction has, it seems to us, been neglected in speaking of him as a draughtsman, and his equipment in this respect has been decided by reference to those of his works in which it is least conspicuous. In his work of pure caricature we cannot obviously expect good drawing, and from the remarks which he makes as to "minute accuracy of design" in his Memoranda on the *Four Stages of Cruelty*, it is clear that he did not intend that any of his cheaper and more popular works should be exhibited as models in this respect. Indeed, it would not be difficult to find in them evidence both of haste and carelessness. That they should tell their story clearly as to action and expression was, in short, all that he desired. But if, on the other hand, he is studied in his best work, say the *Marriage-à-la-Mode* or the *March to Finchley*, it will be found that he rises easily to the occasion, and that he is thoroughly capable, expert, and accurate. The wonderful figure of Viscount Squanderfield in the second picture of *Marriage-à-la-Mode* is a case in point.

The same remarks apply in a measure to his engraving. He did not attempt to compete with Grignion, or Ravenet, or Morellon le Cave. Beauty and delicacy of stroke, he plainly gives us to understand, demanded more patience than he felt disposed to exercise. He regarded the making of fine lines " as a barren and unprofitable study." "The fact is (he declares) that the passions may be more forcibly exprest by a strong bold stroke, than by the most delicate engraving. To expressing them as I felt them, I have paid the utmost attention, and as they were addrest to *hard hearts*, have rather preferred leaving them *hard*, and giving the effect, by a quick touch, to rendering them languid and feeble by fine strokes and soft engraving; which require more care and practice than can often be attained, except by a man of a very quiet turn of mind." All this is manifestly in defence of what he knew to be the assailable side of his work, its occasional lack of finish and haste of execution; and at the same time, it suggests attention to what were its special merits—its spirit, its vigour, its intelligibility.

But it is neither as engraver, draughtsman, nor painter that William Hogarth claims pre-eminence among English artists; it is as a wit, a humourist, a satirist upon canvas. To take some social blot, some fashionable vice, and hold it up sternly to " hard hearts;" to imagine it vividly and dramatically, and body it forth with all the resources of unshrinking realism ; **to** tear away its trappings of convention and prescription, to probe it to the quick, and lay bare all its secret shameful workings to their inevitable end; **to** play upon it with inexhaustible invention, with the keenest and happiest humour; **to decorate it with the utmost** prodigality of fanciful accessory and allusive suggestion; to be conscious at his gravest how the grotesque in life elbows the terrible, **and the** strange grating laugh of Mephistopheles **is** heard through the sorriest story:—these were his gifts, and this was his vocation— a vocation in which he has never yet been rivalled. Let the reader recall for a moment, not indeed such halting competitors as Bunbury and Zoffany, Northcote and the "ingenious" Mr. Penny, but any name of note, which in the last fifty years has been hastily dignified by indulgent criticism with the epithet "Hogarthian," **and then consider** if he honestly believes them to be **on any level with the** painter of *Marriage-à-la-Mode*. **In his own** line he stands supreme and unapproached:—

" Nec viget quidquam simile aut secundum."

CHRONOLOGY OF HOGARTH'S LIFE.

Born in London, Nov. 10	1697
Apprenticed to Ellis Gamble	about 1712-18
Shop-card, " W. Hogarth, Engraver," April 23	1720
Masquerades and Operas (published)	1724
Suit against Morris (*Element of Earth*), May 28	1728
Married Jane Thornhill, March 23	1729
Summer Lodgings at South Lambeth	about 1729
" Five Days' Tour," May 27-31	1732
Summer Lodgings at Isleworth	about 1732
Came to Leicester-Fields	1733
Sir James Thornhill, his father-in-law, died, May 13	1734
Copyright Act (8 Geo. III. cap. 13)	1735
Mother died, June 11	1735
Made **a Governor** and Guardian of the Foundling Hospital	1739
Auction of *Rake's Progress*, &c., February	1745
Journey to **France**	1748 ?
Lottery of *March to Finchley*, April 30	1750
Auction of *Marriage-à-la-Mode*, June 6	1750
" Analysis of Beauty " published, Dec.	1753
Appointed Sergeant-Painter, June **6**	1757
Commenced his duties, July 16	1757
Lady Thornhill died, Nov. 12	1757
Sigismonda painted	before 1761
Re-appointed Sergeant-Painter, **Oct. 30**	1761
Quarrel with Wilkes and Churchill	1762-3
Finis, or *The Bathos*, published, March 3	1764
Died at Leicester Fields, Oct. 25	1764

HOGARTH'S BOOK-PLATE.

A LIST OF ENGRAVINGS BY AND AFTER HOGARTH,

Arranged, as far as possible, according to date of publication.

[N.B.—This list has been mainly compiled from the prints themselves. It does not pretend to record more than a few superficial variations, or to include any but the best known or most important of the artist's works. Exception has, however, been made in favour of several minor plates which illustrate his career. The titles in inverted commas are taken from the engravings.]

	Engraved by
1717 ? The Rape of the Lock. (*Impression from a snuff-box lid. Also reprinted Mar.* 1, 1786) . .	Hogarth.
1720. "W. Hogarth, Engraver, Aprill ye 23rd, 1720." (*Shop-card. We follow the copy in the British Museum*)	Hogarth.
1721 ? An Emblematical Print on the South Sea . .	Hogarth.
"The Lottery"	Hogarth.
1723. Eighteen Plates to the Travels of Aubry de la Motraye	Hogarth.
1724. Dec. 2. "Some of the principal Inhabitants of ye Moon &c.," or Royalty Episcopacy and Law. (*There is a copy by Ireland, dated May* 1, 1788)	Hogarth ?
Seven Plates to Briscoe's "Apuleius" . .	Hogarth.
Masquerades and Operas. Burlington Gate. (*Ireland thinks this the plate which Hogarth calls the* "*Taste of the Town*," v. p. 12) . .	Hogarth.
Frontispiece to Horneck's "Happy Ascetick," 6th edition	Hogarth.

		Engraved by
1725.	Five Prints for the translation of "Cassandra".	Hogarth.
	Fifteen Head-pieces for Beaver's "Roman Military Punishments".	Hogarth.
	"A Just View of the British Stage, or three Heads are better than one. Scene Newgate, by M D-v-to." (*Booth, Wilks, and Cibber contriving a pantomime*)	Hogarth?
	A Satire on the Altar-piece by Kent in St. Clement Danes, Westminster. (*The first impressions were on blue paper*).	Hogarth.
	Berenstat, Cuzzoni, and Senesino. (*Doubtful*).	Hogarth?
1726.	Frontispiece to Amhurst's "Terræ-Filius".	Hogarth.
	Twenty-six figures for Blackwell's "Compendium of Military Discipline".	Hogarth.
	Twelve Prints for Butler's "Hudibras".	Hogarth.
	Seventeen small do.	Hogarth.
	Cuniculari or The Wise Men of Godliman in Consultation. (*A satire on the case of Mary Tofts, the Godalming Rabbit-Breeder*).	Hogarth?
	"The Punishment inflicted on Lemuel Gulliver &c." (*A coarse illustration of a supposed incident in "Gulliver's Travels"*).	Hogarth?
1727.	Music introduc'd to Apollo by Minerva. (*Probably a frontispiece to music*).	Hogarth.
	Masquerade Ticket. (*Generally known as the "large Masquerade Ticket"*).	Hogarth.
	Frontispiece to "A Collection of Songs" by Leveridge.	Hogarth?
1728.	A Ticket for the Benefit of Spiller the Player.	Hogarth?
	Head of Hesiod for Cook's Translation.	Hogarth.
	The "Beggar's Opera" burlesqued.	Hogarth?
1729.	King Henry the Eighth and Anna Bullen. (*Also engraved by T. Cook, Oct. 1, 1801*).	Hogarth.
	Frontispiece to "The Humours of Oxford," a Comedy by the Rev. James Miller.	Vandergucht.
1730.	Frontispiece to "Perseus and Andromeda".	Hogarth.
	Another print of the same, "Perseus descending".	Hogarth.
	Gulliver presented to the Queen of Babilary.	Vandergucht.
1731.	Two Plates to Molière.	**Hogarth.**
	Frontispiece to Fielding's "**Tom Thumb**".	**Vandergucht.**

BY AND AFTER HOGARTH.

Engraved by

1731. Frontispiece to the opera of "The Highland Fair" by Joseph Mitchell . . . . **Vandergucht.**
Taste, or The Man of Taste, or Burlington Gate . . . **Hogarth.**

1732. Ap. 20. Ticket for "Mock Doctor." (*Fielding's Benefit*) . . . . **Hogarth?**
"Rich's Glory or his Triumphant Entry into Covent Garden." (*Doubtful*) . . . . **Hogarth?**

1733. [March]. "Sarah Malcolm," &c. . . . **Hogarth.**
Boys Peeping at Nature. (*Ticket for the "Harlot's Progress;" afterwards used for the "Strolling Actresses" and "Four Times of the Day;" and finally, much altered, for "Moses brought to Pharaoh's Daughter" and "Paul before Felix"*) . . . . **Hogarth.**
A Chorus of Singers. Rehearsal of the oratorio of "Judith" by William Huggins. (*Ticket for "A Midnight Modern Conversation"*) . . **Hogarth.**
A Pleased Audience at a Play, or The Laughing Audience. (*Ticket for "Southwark Fair" and the "Rake's Progress"*) . . . . . **Hogarth.**

1734. Cuzzoni, Farinelli, and Heidegger . . . **Hogarth?**
Frontispiece to Carey's "Chrononhotontologos" **Hogarth?**
"A Harlot's Progress," in six plates. (*All but the first impressions are marked thus* †) . . **Hogarth.**
"A Midnight Modern Conversation." (*Some of the impressions are in red*) . . . . **Hogarth.**

1735. June 25. A Rake's Progress, in eight plates. (*The last plate was "Retouched by the Author 1763." A group was also added to Pl. iv., 2nd state*) . **Hogarth.**
Southwark Fair. (*Dated 1733; but not published until 1735*) . . . . **Hogarth.**
A Woman swearing a Child to a grave Citizen. (*There is also a mezzotint, dated June, 1816, by James Young*) . . . . } **J. Sympson, Jun.**

1736. Mar. 3. The Distressed Poet. (*Afterwards issued, Dec. 15, 1740, with variations*) . . . **Hogarth.**
Mar. 3. "The Company of Undertakers," or A Consultation of Physicians . . . . **Hogarth.**
April 25. A Ticket for Fielding's Benefit in "Pasquin" . . . . **Hogarth.**

A LIST OF ENGRAVINGS

Engraved by

1736. Oct. 26. The Sleeping Congregation. ("*Retouched and Improved April* 21, 1762") . . . Hogarth.
Dec. 15. Before and After . . . . . Hogarth.
"Tartuff's Banquet" . . . . . . Vandergucht.
Right Hon. Frances Lady Byron. (*Mezzotint*) . J. Faber, Jun.
Frontispiece to Grimston's Comedy of "The Lawyer's Fortune, or Love in a Hollow Tree" Hogarth?
1737. Jan. 20, 173$. Scholars at a Lecture. (*The second state is dated Mar.* 3, 1736) . . . . Hogarth.
Æneas in a Storm. (*Satire on George II. Doubtful*) Hogarth.
1738. Mar 25. The Four Times of the Day. (*In some impressions of "Evening," which Baron engraved, the face of the woman was printed in red to indicate heat, and the hands of the man in blue to show his trade of a dyer*) . . . . . } Hogarth and B. Baron.
Mar. 25. Strolling Actresses dressing in a Barn Hogarth.
Eight Plates to Jarvis's "Don Quixote" . . Hogarth.
Sancho's Feast . . . . Hogarth.
1739. The Foundlings. (*Head-piece to Power of Attorney*) . . . . Le Cave.
1741. Nov. 30. "The Enraged Musician" . . . Hogarth.
1742. "Martin Folkes, Esq." (*Also engraved in the same year in mezzotint by J. Faber, Jun.*) . Hogarth.
The Mystery of Masonry brought to Light by ye Gormagons . . . . Hogarth.
1743. "Dr. Benjamin Hoadly, Lord Bishop of Winchester" . . . . B. Baron.
"Characters" and "Caricaturas." (*Subscription Ticket to the "Marriage-à-la-Mode"*) . . Hogarth.
(*Before.*) Gustavus, Viscount Boyne. (*Mezzotint*) M. Ford.
1745. The Battle of the Pictures. (*A Ticket for the Auction of the "Rake's Progress," etc., in February,* 1745, *v. p.* 46) . . . . . Hogarth.
Ap. 1. "Marriage A-la-Mode" in six Plates. (*Pl. i. and vi. engraved by G. Scotin; Pl. ii. and iii. by B. Baron; Pl. iv. and v. by Ravenet. It was also engraved by B. Earlom in mezzotint, June* 4, 1795—*Aug.* 1, 1800) . . . Scotin, &c.
Mask and Palette. (*Subscription Ticket to "Garrick in Richard III."*) . . . . . Hogarth.

A PLEASED AUDIENCE AT A PLAY.

		Engraved by
1746.	May 24. "Taste in High Life." (*Also engraved by S. Phillips, May 1*, 1798)	—
	June 20. "M*r*. Garrick in the Character of Richard the 3*d*." (*There is also a mezzotint by A. Miller, Dublin*, 1746)	{ Hogarth and C. Grignion.
	Aug. 25. "Simon Lord Lovat"	Hogarth.
	Arms, Bagpipes, &c. (*Subscription Ticket to "March to Finchley"*)	Hogarth.
1747.	Sept. 30. "Industry and Idleness", in Twelve plates	Hogarth.
	[Dec. 5.] Head-piece to the "Jacobite's Journal"	—
	The Stage-Coach, or Country Inn Yard . .	Hogarth.
	"Jacobus Gibbs, Architectus, 1747." (*There is also a mezzotint by McArdell*)	B. Baron.
1748.	Hymen and Cupid. (*Ticket for the "Masque of Alfred"*)	—
	Mr. Ranby's House at Chiswick	Hogarth.
1749.	Mar. 6. "O the Roast Beef of Old England etc.," or the Gate of Calais	} Hogarth and C. Mosley.
	"Captain Thomas Coram." (*This was a mezzotint. The picture was also engraved by W. Nutter, Dec.* 1, 1796)	McArdell.
	John Palmer, Esq.	B. Baron.
	"Gulielmus Hogarth." His own Portrait with Pug Dog. (*Engraved also by B. Smith, June* 4, 1795)	Hogarth.
1750.	Dec. 30. "A Representation of the March of the Guards towards Scotland in the Year 1745," or The March to Finchley. (*The plate was at first dated Dec. 30, a Sunday, and afterwards altered to Dec. 31st. There are other notable variations*)	L. Sullivan.
1751.	Feb. 1. "Beer Street." (*In the first state the blacksmith lifts up a Frenchman by the waist-belt; in the second a shoulder of mutton is substituted*) .	Hogarth.[1]
	Feb. 1. "Gin Lane"	Hogarth.[1]
	„ The Four Stages of Cruelty . . .	Hogarth.[1]

---

[1] These **six** prints only bear the words "Design'd by W. Hogarth." But see his "Memoranda" in J. Ireland, iii. p. 355.

A LIST OF ENGRAVINGS

		Engraved by
1751.	May 1. "Paul before Felix." (*Burlesqued*)	Hogarth.
1752.	Feb. 5. Paul before Felix	Hogarth.
	Paul before Felix. (*Altered*)	L. Sullivan.
	Moses brought to Pharaoh's Daughter	Hogarth and L. Sullivan.
	Columbus breaking the Egg. (*Subscription Ticket to the "Analysis of Beauty"*)	Hogarth.
1753.	Mar. 5. Two Plates to the "Analysis of Beauty"	Hogarth.
	Frontispiece to Kirby's "Perspective"	L. Sullivan.
1754.	Crowns, Mitres, etc. (*Subscription Ticket to the "Election Entertainment"*)	Hogarth.
1755.	Four Prints of an Election. (*Pl. i. by Hogarth, dated Feb. 24, 1755; pl. ii. by C. Grignion, dated Feb. 20, 1757; pl. iii. by Hogarth and Le Cave, dated Feb. 20, 1758; and pl. iv. by Hogarth and F. Aviline, dated Jan. 1, 1758*	Hogarth, &c.
1756.	Mar. 8. "France" and "England," or "The Invasion"	Hogarth.
	(*Before.*) John Pine, in imitation of Rembrandt. (*Mezzotint*)	J. McArdell.
1758.	Sept. 4. "The Bench"	Hogarth.
	Hogarth painting the Comic Muse. (*The latest impressions bear the inscription "W. Hogarth, 1764," and the face and mask of Comedy are marked with black*).	Hogarth (*in part*).
1759.	Nov. 5. The Cockpit	Hogarth.
	Frontispiece to vols. ii. and iv. of "Tristram Shandy"	Ravenet.
1760.	Frontispiece to Kirby's "Perspective of Architecture".	W. Woollett.
	"Mr. Huggins".	Major.
1761.	May 7. Frontispiece and Tailpiece to Artists' Catalogue	C. Grignion.
	Oct. 15. "The Five Orders of Periwigs, etc."	Hogarth.
	Time Smoking a Picture. (*Subscription Ticket to "Sigismunda"*)	Hogarth.
1762.	Mar. 15. "Credulity, Superstition, and Fanaticism, a Medley"	Hogarth.
	Sept. 7. "The Times, Pl. i."	Hogarth.

Page 118.

		Engraved by
1762.	Frontispiece to the " Farmer's Return," by Garrick	Basire.
	" T. Morell, S.T.P.—S.S.A."	Basire.
	" Henry Fielding, Ætatis 48."	Basire.
1763.	May 16. " John Wilkes, Esqr."	Hogarth.
	Aug. 1. " The Bruiser, C. Churchill, etc." (*The second state has a tablet added in the corner, see p.* 97)	Hogarth.
	Frontispiece to Clubbe's " Physiognomy "	L. Sullivan.
1764.	Mar. 3. " The Bathos, or Manner of Sinking in Sublime Paintings, inscribed to the Dealers in Dark Pictures." (*See p.* 98)	Hogarth.
1767.	Satan, Sin, and Death	C. Townley.
1772.	Feb. 24. " The Good Samaritan "	Ravenet and Delatre.
	" The Pool of Bethesda "	Ravenet and Picot.
1775.	Oct. 31. " The Politician ".	J. K. Sherwin.
1781.	May 14. Four Heads from the Hampton Court Cartoons	Hogarth.
	June. His own Portrait. (*Begun by Wheltdon and finished by himself. Mezzotint*)	C. Townley.
	July 31. " Arms for the Foundling Hospital," 1747	R. Livesay.
	Nov. 27. " M^r. Gabriel Hunt "	R. Livesay.
	" M^r. Ben. Read "	R. Livesay.
	Nine Prints for Hogarth's " Tour "	R. Livesay.
1782.	Feb. 1. " The Staymaker "	J. Haynes.
	" Debates on Palmistry "	J. Haynes.
	Mar. 19. Henry Fox, Lord Holland	J. Haynes.
	" James Caulfield, Earl of Charlemont	J. Haynes.
	Mar. 25. " Shrimps ! "	F. Bartolozzi.
	Ap. 23. " Hogarth's Crest." (*See p.* 99)	R. Livesay.
	Aug. 1. Eta Beta PY. (*Invitation Card*)	J. Cary.
1786.	Mar. 1. Orator Henley Christening a Child	Jane Ireland.
	" Wm. Hogarth "—his own Portrait in a Wig	S. Ireland.
	Miss Rich	M. Knight.
1788.	Feb. 8. Jenny Cameron	—
1790.	May 29. " The Times, Pl. ii."	Hogarth.
	July 1. " Beggar's Opera, Act iii."	W. Blake.

A LIST OF ENGRAVINGS.

		Engraved by
1792. Jan. 1. " The Indian Emperor"	. . .	R. Dodd.
1793. Feb. 1. " Sigismunda." (*Mezzotint.* There is another engraving by *B. Smith*, dated June 4, 1795. *It had also been partly etched by Basire*)		Dunkarton.
1794. Jan. 1. Sealing the Sepulchre	. . . .	I. Jenner.
„ The Sepulchre	. . . .	I. Jenner.
Sir James Thornhill	. . . . .	S. Ireland.
Justice Welch	. . . . .	S. Ireland.
Theodore Gardelle	. . . .	S. Ireland.
1795. Nov. 12. " Hogarth's First Thought for the Medley ", or Enthusiasm Delineated	. .	I. Mills.
1797. June 1. " Lavinia Fenton, Duchess of Bolton"	.	S. Apostool.
" M^{rs}. Hogarth "	. . . .	Ryder.
1799. Mar. 13. " The Savoyard Girl"	. . .	G. Sherlock.
May 1. " Rosamonds Pond"	. . .	Merigot.
„ " Falstaff examining his Recruits"		Ryder.
„ " Lady Thornhill "	. . .	Le Cœur.
„ " M^r. Thornhill "	. . . .	Whesell.
" Scene at a Banking House " [Child's]	.	Barlow.
1803. June 1. " Bambridge on Trial for Murder &c."	.	T. Cook.
Nov. 1. The House of Commons	. .	A. Fogg.
1804. " Royal Masquerade, Somerset House"	. .	T. Cook.
1809. Mar. 1. Joseph Porter, Esq.	. . .	T. Cook.
A Musical Study	. . . .	T. Cook.
Hogarth's Painting Room	. . . .	T. Cook.
1820. May. James Thomson (*Lithograph*)	. .	M. Gauci.
June. John Gay. (*Lithograph*)	. .	M. Gauci.
1821. Ap. 4. Handel	. . . . .	C. Turner.
1825. " The Lady's Last Stake"	. . . .	Cheesman.
1837. " Charity in the Cellar"	. . . .	Leney.
1840. Dec. 25. " View in St. James's Park shewing Rosamond's Pond." (*Lithograph*)	. .	F. Ross.
1842. Mar. 25. John Broughton, Prize Fighter. (*Lithograph*)	. . . . .	F. Ross.
" Garrick and his Wife." (*See p.* 64)	.	H. Bourne.
Daniel Lock, Esq., F.S.A. (*Mezzotint*)	.	J. McArdell.
" A Sea Officer." (*Sir A. Schomberg*)	.	J. Flight.

A LIST OF THE PRINCIPAL PAINTINGS BY HOGARTH,

Arranged Chronologically.

[N.B.—Many pictures not included in this list have been exhibited at the "Old Masters" and other exhibitions; and of some of those here given there are *replicas* in different collections. With exception of a few which it has been possible to correct accurately, the dates are taken from J. B. Nichols; but it will be obvious that where they correspond with those of the engravings *some earlier date* should generally be ascribed to the pictures. A complete catalogue of Hogarth's paintings and sketches is a desideratum, but it cannot be attempted here.]

		Present Possessor.
1729.	Committee of House of Commons examining Bambridge	Earl of Carlisle.
	Scene in the "Beggar's Opera"	John Murray, Esq.
	Scene in the "Beggar's Opera." (*Another*)	Duke of Leeds.
	Scene in the "Beggar's Opera." (*Another*)	Louis Huth, Esq.
1730.	Before and After	—
	Before and After. (*Another*)	Frederick Locker, Esq.
(?)	The Politician	—
1731.	Scene in the "Indian Emperor"	Holland House.
1733.	Sarah Malcolm	—[1]
	Southwark Fair	Burnt in 1807.
1733-4.	A Harlot's Progress	Five burnt at Fonthill, 1755.[2]

---

[1] This picture is now (1879) at Mr. Cox's, 57, Pall Mall.
[2] The sixth (Picture 2) belongs to the Earl of Wemyss.

		Present Possessor.
1733-4.	A Harlot's Progress. (*Two Pictures from Novar Collection*)	Earl of Rosebery.
1734.	A Midnight Modern Conversation [1]	—
1735.	Woman swearing a Child to a grave Citizen [2]	—
	A Rake's Progress	Soane Museum.
	A Distressed Poet	Duke of Westminster.
1736.	The Pool of Bethesda	St. Bartholomew's Hospital.
	The Good Samaritan	St. Bartholomew's Hospital.
1738.	Strolling Actresses dressing in a Barn	Burnt at Littleton, in 1874.
	The Four Times of the Day [3]	—
1739.	Captain Coram	Foundling Hospital.
1741.	The Enraged Musician	—
	Martin Folkes	Royal Society.
1742.	Taste in High Life	—
1745.	The Marriage-à-la-Mode	National Gallery.
1745.	Hogarth with Pug-dog	National Gallery.
1746.	Garrick as Richard III.	Earl of Feversham.
	Simon Lord Lovat	National Portrait Gallery.
	Simon Lord Lovat (*Another*)	H. Graves, Esq.
	Mary Hogarth	National Gallery.
1748.	Paul before Felix	Society of Lincoln's Inn.[4]
1749.	The Gate of Calais	Family of H. F. Bolckow, Esq.
1750.	The March to Finchley	Foundling Hospital.
1752.	Moses brought to Pharaoh's Daughter	Foundling Hospital.
1755.	The Election Series	Soane Museum.
1756.	Altar-piece, St. Mary Redcliffe	Fine Arts Society at Clifton.
1758.	Hogarth painting the Comic Muse	National Portrait Gallery.
1759.	The Lady's Last Stake	Louis Huth, Esq.
1760.	Sigismonda	National Gallery.
	A View of the Green Park, 1760	Earl Spencer.

---

[1] There are versions of this picture at Basildon and at the Earl of Egremont's at Petworth.

[2] There is a copy in the South Kensington Museum by J. Collet.

[3] "Night" belongs or belonged to Lady Taunton.

[4] See letter at pp. 72, 73.

PRINCIPAL PAINTINGS BY HOGARTH.   123

UNCERTAIN DATE.

	Present Possessor.
Falstaff reviewing his Recruits	Family of H. F. Bolckow, Esq.
Shrimp Girl	Sir Philip Miles.
A View in St. James's Park	Louisa, Lady Ashburton.
James Gibbs, Architect	St. Martin's-in-the-Fields.
Mrs. Hogarth	H. Bingham Mildmay, Esq.
Garrick and his Wife	Royal Collection.
Mrs. Garrick	Earl of Dunmore.
Lavinia Fenton, Duchess of Bolton	C. Brinsley Marlay, Esq.
Lavinia Fenton as "Polly Peachum"	Sir Philip Miles.
Miss Rich	C. H. Hawkins, Esq.
Dr. Arnold, of Ashby Lodge	Fitzwilliam Museum.
Miss Arnold, of Ashby Lodge	Fitzwilliam Museum.
Ashby Lodge [1]	Fitzwilliam Museum.
Mrs. Elizabeth Hoadly	Ernest Gye, Esq.
Sir C. Hawkins	Royal College of Surgeons.
Peg Woffington	Marquis of Lansdowne.
William, fifth Duke of Devonshire	Lord Chesham.
Hon. J. Hamilton	Duke of Abercorn.
The Country in the Olden Time	Ayscough Fawkes, Esq.

[1] By Hogarth or Richard Wilson.

ORIGINAL PRICES OF HOGARTH'S PRINTS.

(*From Nichols's "Anecdotes," 1781.*)

Prints *published by the late* W. HOGARTH: *Genuine Impressions of which are to be had of* Mrs. HOGARTH, *at her House in* Leicester Fields, 1781.

	£	s.	d.
Frontispiece	0	3	0
Harlot's Progress, in six prints	1	1	0
Rake's Progress, in eight prints	2	2	0
Marriage-à-la-mode, in six prints	1	11	6
Four Times of the Day, in four prints	1	0	0
Before and After, two prints	0	5	0
Midnight Conversation	0	5	0
Distress'd Poet	0	3	0
Enraged Musician	0	3	0
Southwark Fair	0	5	0
Mr. Garrick in the Character of King Richard III.	0	7	6
Calais, or the Roast Beef of Old England	0	5	0
Paul before Felix	0	7	6
Ditto, with Alterations	0	6	0
Moses brought to Pharaoh's Daughter	0	7	6
March to Finchley	0	10	6
Strolling Actresses dressing in a barn	0	5	0
Four Prints of an Election	2	2	0
Bishop of Winchester	0	3	0
The Effects of Idleness and Industry, exemplified in the Conduct of two Fellow-Prentices, in twelve prints	0	12	0
Lord Lovat	0	1	0
Sleeping Congregation	0	1	0
Country-Inn Yard	0	1	0

ORIGINAL PRICES OF HOGARTH'S PRINTS.

	£	s.	d.
Paul before Felix, in the Manner of Rembran[d]t	0	5	0
Various Characters of Heads, in five groups	0	2	6
Columbus breaking the Egg	0	1	0
The Bench	0	1	6
Beer Street and Gin Lane, two prints	0	3	0
Four Stages of Cruelty, four prints	0	6	0
Two prints of an Invasion	0	2	0
A Cock Match	0	3	0
The Five Orders of Periwigs	0	1	0
The Medley	0	5	0
The Times	0	2	0
Wilkes	0	1	0
Bruiser	0	1	6
Finis	0	2	6

N.B.—Any Person purchasing the whole together **may have them deliver'd bound, at the Price of Thirteen Guineas; a sufficient Margin will be left for Framing.**

Where likewise may be had,

The ANALYSIS of BEAUTY, in Quarto, with two explanatory Prints, Price 15 Shillings.

INDEX.

	Page
Altar-piece of St. Mary Redcliffe	83
"Analysis of Beauty"	75, 76, 77, 99
Apuleius, Illustrations to	12
Artists' Catalogue, Designs for	89, 90
Bambridge, Examination of	15
Baron, the Engraver	47
Bates, William	99
Bathos, The	98, 99
Battle of the Pictures	46, 47
Beer Street	71
Beggar's Opera, Scene from	15
Bench, The	84, 99
Bourne, Vincent	30
Boys Peeping at Nature	24
"Britophil," Hogarth's nom de plume	36
Bruiser, The	96, 97
Burlesque on Kent	12, 13
Burlington Gate	16
Canvassing for Votes	79
Carestini, the Singer	49, 54
Cary, Rev. H. F.	102, 103
Cassandra, Prints for	12
Chairing of the Members	81
Charteris, Colonel	23
"Chrononhotontologos"	30
Churchill, Charles	62, 93, 94, 95, 96, 97
Cock, the Auctioneer	56, 58
Cockpit, The	85
Columbus breaking the Egg	79
Commentators, Hogarth's	1, 2
Company of Undertakers	35
Consultation of Physicians	35
Conversation paintings	14, 20
Cook, Dutton	102
Coram, Captain	20, 41, 42
Coram, Captain, Portrait of	42
Country Dance	78
Country Inn Yard	65, 66
Cowper	39, 40, 43
Credulity, Superstition, and Fanaticism	75, 91, 93
Crowns, Mitres, &c.	25, 79
Cuzzoni, Farinelli, and Heidegger	50
Dalton, James, highwayman	23
Dashwood, Sir Francis	62
Desaguiliers, Dr.	36
Distrest Poet	35, 43, 44
Don Quixote, Illustrations to	42
Draper, Edward	39

INDEX.

	Page
Election Entertainment	79
Election Prints	75
Enraged Musician	35, 43, 44
Enthusiasm Delineated	91, 92
Farinelli, the Singer	30, 31
"**Farmer's** Return"	64
Fielding, Henry	16, 31, 39, 62, 98
Fielding's Benefit, Ticket for	35
Finis, or the Bathos	98
"Five Days Peregrination"	17, 18
Folkes, Martin, *Portrait of*	42
Ford, Rev. **Cornelius**	30
Forrest, **E.**	17
Forrest, **Theodosius**	17 (note), 69
Foundling **Hospital**	41, 42
Foundlings, *The*	41
Four Stages of Cruelty	71
Four Times of the Day	15, 34, 38, 45
Gamble, Ellis, Shop-card of	8, 9
Garrick, David	62, 63, 84, 96
Garrick as Richard III.	63
Garrick and his Wife	64
Gate of Calais, The	68
Gilpin, Rev. Mr.	58
Gin Lane	71
Goldsmith, Oliver	38, 43, 62
Gonson, Sir John	23
Good Samaritan	33, 34
Gostling, The **Rev. Mr.**	18
Gray, the Poet	62
Happy Marriage	59
Harlot's Progress	21, 25, 45
Henley, Orator	30
Henry VIII. and Anna Bullen	15
Hicks, **N. T.**	103
Hoadly, Bishop, *Portrait of*	44
Hoadlys, **The**	61

	Page
Hogarth, Portraits of	104
Hogarth, William, of Aberdeen	104
Hogarth's **Book** Plate	112
Hogarth's **Crest**	99
Hogarth's Engravings, **List** of	113
Hogarth's Haunts	61
Hogarth's House at Chiswick	102, 103, 104
Hogarth's Shop-card	11
Hogarth's Tomb	100, 104
Hogarth's Will	100
Hudibras, Illustrations to	12, 13
Indian Emperor, The	15
Industry and *Idleness*	66
Invasion, **The**	84
Jacobite's Journal, Head-piece to	67
Johnson, **Dr.**	62
Kendal **Arms**	11
Kent, William	12, 13
King, Dr. Arnold	62
King, Moll, Portrait of	39
Lady's **Last** Stake, The	86, 89
Lambert, the Scene-painter	20
Lane, Mr., of Hillingdon	58, 59
Large Masquerade Ticket	16
Laughing Audience	26
Lewis, Mary	102, 103, 105
London, Hogarth's	5
Lottery, The	12
Lovat, Lord, Portrait of	65
Malcolm, Sarah	24
Man of Taste, The	16
Manuscripts, Hogarth	7, 18, 68
Mapp, Sarah, Bonesetter	35
March to Finchley	70

Marriage-à-la-Mode	47
Masquerades and Operas	12, 14, 25
Midnight Modern Conversation .	30
Misaubin, Dr.	23, 54
Mitchell, the Poet	20
Morell, Dr.	62, 98
Moses brought to Pharaoh's Daughter	71, 72
"Musical Entertainer," Bickham's	30 (note)
Needham, Mother	23, 92
Northcote.	67
Opera House, 1735	30
Paul before Felix . . .	71, 72
Paul before Felix (Burlesque) .	73
Picquet	86, 89
Pine, the Engraver . . .	20, 69
Piozzi, Mrs.	62, 87
Piracy of Prints, Act to prevent	25
Pleased Audience at a Play . .	26
Politician, The	15
Polling, The	81
Pool of Bethesda	33, 34
Rake's Progress	25, 45
Ralph, Mr.	62
Rape of the Lock	11
Ravenet, the Engraver . . .	47
Richardson, Samuel . . .	62
Rich's Glory	16
Roast Beef of Old England .	68, 69
Roubilliac's Bust of Hogarth .	105
Runciman, the Painter . .	102
St. Bartholomew's Hospital .	33, 34
Sala, G. A.	2, 57
Sales by Auction . . .	45, 47, 58

Scholars at a Lecture	35
Scotin, the Engraver	47
Scott, the Landscape Painter .	17
Shebbeare, Dr.	82
Sigismonda . . .	63, 75, 87, 89
Sleeping Congregation . . .	36
Somervile	31
South Sea, Emblematic Print on	11
Southwark Fair	29
Spring Gardens Exhibition . .	89
Stage Coach, The	65
Statuary's Yard	78, 79
Steevens, George . . .	2, 105
Stephens, F. G. . .	2, 29, 54, 77
Strolling Actresses in a Barn	35, 40, 45
Swift	31, 46, 104
Taste in High Life	44
Taste of the Town, The .	12, 13, 25
Terræ-Filius, Frontispiece . .	12
Thackeray	39, 44
Thornhill, Sir James	24, 31, 36, 102
Thornhill, John	17, 85
Time Smoking a Picture . . .	88
Times, The (Pl. i.) . .	93, 94, 97
Times, The (Pl. 2)	97
Tom Thumb, Frontispiece . .	16
Tothall, the Draper	17
Townley, Mr.	62
Walpole, Horace .	1, 41, 58, 75, 89
Wanstead Assembly . . .	15, 78
Warburton, Bishop	62
Ward, Dr.	23
Weideman, the Flute-player .	56
Weighing House, The	93
Welch, Mr. Justice	70
Wilkes, John	59, 62, 93, 94, 95, 97

www.ingramcontent.com/pod-product-compliance
Lightning Source LLC
Chambersburg PA
CBHW020303170426
43202CB00008B/477